Praise for
From Tension to Transformation

"In *From Tension to Transformation*, Janet M. Harvey serves as your guide to lead generative change. Amidst all of the chaos, leaders who rely on empowering reflection—available through the generative vehicle for change that this book offers—can look ahead and see a year filled with ongoing learning, improved collaboration, and better results."

—Mark Thompson, Chairman, ChiefExecutiveAlliance.com

"Pragmatic, provocative, fully actionable, and so urgently needed in today's VUCA world. In *From Tension to Transformation: A Leader's Guide to Generative Change,* Janet Harvey taps into, and offers, a thoroughly researched and practical guide for embracing and managing the ever-present and cascading tensions confronting today's leaders. Whether a senior, experienced leader, an emerging leader, or a leader in mid-stride, *From Tension to Transformation* is a must-read. If you are honest with yourself, you will see painfully clear, or amusingly faint, glimmers of yourself in every chapter.

Thankfully, I see myself in all three. Do not miss this transformative and generative read."

—Michael D. Rochelle, PCC, CMC, LTG (USA, retired)

"Extraordinary leaders actively pursue lifelong learning, introspection, and increasing insight. *From Tension to Transformation* brims with authentic and practical wisdom—consider it an essential companion on the leadership journey."

—Laura S. Kaiser, FACHE, President and CEO, SSM Health

"In this increasingly fast-changing world leaders need to build trust more than ever by being trustworthy. This in turn requires congruence of thoughts, feelings, and actions. Janet's new book shows a roadmap to accomplish this. A must-read for leaders navigating unprecedented change."

—Niren Chaudhary, Chairman of the Board, Panera Brands

"Janet Harvey shares with us the opportunity for guided personal reflection with *From Tension to Transformation: A Leader's Guide to Generative Change*. She asks us to tap and reclaim our sovereignty to bring our best to all aspects of our lives and to pause (maybe even slow down!) to be with tension, judgment, and fear so we can grow and just 'be' with more intention. This is not a book to be read. Rather, it is journey guide to being and bringing all of you to life—personal and professional. Enjoy the work!"

—Shannon Connor Phillips, MD, Chief Health Officer, Joyous

"Janet Harvey is an unignorable voice in the social impact leadership space and with *From Tension to Transformation*, she has raised the bar again. She destroys antiquated thinking with aplomb and forces the reader to rethink their beliefs about effective leadership, the pitfalls of speed, and the power of generative change. This book should be required reading in all MBA & executive leadership programs worldwide."

—Alok Appadurai, Founder and CEO, Uplift Millions

"If, like me, you have spent most of your working life as a sales leader charging at a moving target we call business growth and rarely having time to pause and reflect, then *From Tension to Transformation: A Leader's Guide to Generative Change* by Janet M. Harvey is the book for you. Reading and reflecting on the lessons shared by a master coach will help you to sit with the fear of inactivity that can lead us to make rash judgments before thoroughly considering all the implications. Managed properly, tension can be healthy, confrontation can be constructive, and fear can be harnessed—this ground-breaking work shows you how."

—Kevin Thiele, Founder and CEO, Sales Code

"*From Tension to Transformation* will activate the fearless intuitive leader inside of you. Janet Harvey provides the language and reading experience to turn fear and judgement into valuable means to rediscover our connection with the body, heart, and head, effectively deepening our capacity to remain calm and centered as we navigate the ever-increasing demands of today's challenges."

—Chris Mijatovich, Strategic life coach, Commercial supply chain manager, New Energies at Shell

"I love how this book is written, where each topic can stand on its own or be read in the order they were written. Janet Harvey is shining a light on a new way of leading that is more thoughtful and productive. In *From Tension to Transformation*, Janet challenges today's leaders to embrace judgment and differences in ways they never have before, especially in the workplace. *From Tension to Transformation* helps business owners answer some of the most important questions that have emerged since the pandemic."

—Rev. Esther Alley, ICF professional certified coach

"Both in life and in business, we often spend a lot of time and resources making progress, but at times making the wrong kind of progress. Janet challenges us to stop and reflect, so we don't waste our lives. Her work allows us to see fear, doubt, self-critique, tension, and discomfort, not as problems to be solved, but as realities necessary for greatness. If you want to achieve your own greatness, *From Tension to Transformation* is your personal Yoda—a companion for self-reflection and a tool to roadmap your path to greatness."

—Ben Owden, LD trainer and workplace culture consultant

"To begin, you must look within—and Janet is the perfect example of a leader who preaches what she practices, and practices what she preaches. Her words inspire you to practice self-reflection, and I firmly believe that *From Tension to Transformation* will help you to grow both personally and professionally."

—Craig M. Chavis Jr., Award-winning author and founder, Solo Creator Club

"Brilliant! As always, Janet provides us with such amazing learning and wisdom. *From Tension to Transformation: A Leader's Guide to Generative Change* is no exception. She helps us understand what it means for us to be sovereign. Her wonderfully told story and exercises for learning how to honor our intuition help us challenge ourselves and grow as leaders. And we are all leaders!"

—Garry Schleifer, CEO and publisher, *Choice Magazine*

"There are many theorists answering the call to help leaders manage the complexities of our time. In this extraordinary book, *From Tension to Transformation*, Janet Harvey goes a step further. She brings in the heart, and courage, and she gives leaders the ability to make meaning of chaos so that they can respond to any crisis from a centered and chosen place. This remarkable and truly transformative work is both imaginative and hugely practical, and its ideas will help you reshape your organization by deepening your own life."

—**Laurence Hillman, PhD, Co-Founder, Archetypes At Work**

from
TENSION
to
TRANSFORMATION

from

TENSION

to TRANSFORMATION

A LEADER'S GUIDE TO GENERATIVE CHANGE

JANET M. HARVEY

Advantage | Books

Published by Advantage Books, Charleston, South Carolina.
An imprint of Advantage Media.

ADVANTAGE is a registered trademark, and the Advantage colophon is a trademark of Advantage Media Group, Inc.

Printed in the United States of America.

10 9 8 7 6 5 4 3 2 1

ISBN: 978-1-64225-918-6 (Paperback)
ISBN: 978-1-64225-917-9 (eBook)

Library of Congress Control Number: 2023922012

Cover design by Wesley Strickland.
Layout design by Megan Elger.

This publication is designed to provide accurate and authoritative information in regard to the subject matter covered. It is sold with the understanding that the publisher is not engaged in rendering legal, accounting, or other professional services. If legal advice or other expert assistance is required, the services of a competent professional person should be sought.

Advantage Books is an imprint of Advantage Media Group. Advantage Media helps busy entrepreneurs, CEOs, and leaders write and publish a book to grow their business and become the authority in their field. Advantage authors comprise an exclusive community of industry professionals, idea-makers, and thought leaders. For more information go to **advantagemedia.com**.

For my husband, Russell, who still wonders how it is that I wake up each day with a smiling heart and zest for what's to come. This book is possible because of your partnership in our lives and the champion you are every moment for my generative work in the world. I love you!

CONTENTS

ACKNOWLEDGMENTS

I owe everything I've learned and shared in this book to the more than twelve thousand hours I've spent with leaders and their teams from around the world who chose to lead organizations of all sizes, and types of industries and missions. Each person who courageously engaged in self-learning and boldly stepped into a fuller expression of themselves than they thought possible, generated more excellence, more joy, and more love for the thousands of people they led.

My knowledge of this positive ripple that arises from generative coaching solutions has fueled my commitment to coaching and the experience of bliss through my work every day. It is their stories, their experiences, their learning, growth, and change, that makes this book a timeless resource and a salute to the legacy of leading from sovereignty.

INTRODUCTION

It's not that I'm so smart, it's just that I stay with problems longer.
—ALBERT EINSTEIN, THEORETICAL PHYSICIST

Tension in the workplace is inevitable. If you're in a leadership role, you've likely noticed that the intensity of that tension, as well as the frequency with which thorny problems arise, is growing. If you don't identify as a leader in your current role, consider this: everybody is a leader, at the least of themselves. Leading yourself well is the first step to leading others well, too.

As an executive coach with twenty-seven-plus years of experience, this suggests one thing to me: we all could get better at being comfortable with the discomfort and *sitting* in that tension just a little bit longer. The pace and complexity of cascading crises in modern business require a fresh approach. This book explores the vehicle for generative change as one right answer to consider.

Generative change is something I've been researching for over a decade. I first began my qualitative research into the topic in 2012, because people kept asking me, "Why does what you do *work*?" Actually, what they were most frequently asking me was, "Why do you make my head hurt?" That's the key: this technique works *because* it makes people's heads hurt—*because* it causes them to slow down, think carefully, and communicate more clearly to their teams so that they can produce better, more valuable results.

Most leaders assume they already know how to do that. After all, you wouldn't have made it to a leadership position if you didn't know how to lead in a way that produces results, right? But ask yourself: *Do I always get the results I want? If I'm not consistently getting the results I want, what's getting in the way? Have I ever tried to address the thing that's getting in the way?*

When I have these conversations with the CEOs and executive team members I coach, some get angry—because I'm challenging their beliefs about who they are and what they do. That's OK. That's at the crux of what effective coaching does: it challenges people's beliefs, assumptions, biases, and preferences and invites them to act in a more conscious and deliberate way so that they can lead more effectively.

I also recognize that anger usually comes from a place of fear. I have a philosophy that our fear is protecting what we hold most dear. That's often our sense of self. I've found that most leaders adopt an expected identity, both to achieve and to avoid feeling uncomfortable. Shaking that identity, even for the better, creates tension. How can leaders learn to sit in that tension and leverage it for positive change? The answer lies in an unexpected place: judgment.

Why I Embrace Judgment— and Suggest You Do, Too

Fear and judgment go hand in hand. We judge what is different from us and fear it. At the same time, all of us know the ugly feeling of being judged for our difference. We are biologically predisposed to judge, especially when we experience something different from us.

Our judgments speak to a biological need to stay safe and belong. Judgment is natural, and I see no use in disavowing it. The key is learning how to leverage judgment—how to take this instinct to judge and harness it to lead us to a state of wonder, openness, and sovereignty.

I am no stranger to judgment. I was confronted with it at a young age. My parents told me I was "just like every other kid." This was a well-intentioned falsehood that was quickly debunked on my first day of kindergarten, when a boy pointed at me and said, "Who let the red skin in?" Snickers followed. I was born with a large port-wine mark on the left side of my face. I didn't fully understand what "red skin" meant at the time, but I knew that the boy's words were meant to hurt me (and they did).

> **The key is learning how to leverage judgment—how to take this instinct to judge and harness it to lead us to a state of wonder, openness, and sovereignty.**

That day told me that I was different and that my difference would provoke judgment. I've been judged by others many times since then. When I was in my twenties, I had a part-time job cold-calling for brokers at a financial services firm, then named Shearson Lehman. I was actually very good at it—so good that one of the brokers suggested that I talk to the branch manager about going on full-time. What followed was my first conscious experience of misogyny.

My interview with the branch manager hadn't even really begun—he'd barely asked me a question—when he got up from his chair, came around the desk, and looked me over, checking out my legs and my breasts. I looked up at him and said, "What the hell are you doing?" to which he replied, "You're not pretty enough to be here." I asked, "So the fact that I've produced more business in the portfolios of the brokers I support than anybody else who does my role doesn't matter? You're not interested in investing in my talent?" He said, "No, I could easily replace you." Today, I'd have some choice words for that man. Back then, I didn't know what to say.

> **Think of a time when you felt judged by another. How did you react in that moment? What feelings does that memory stir up now?**

In the moment, those instances of judgment sting. But I also see the value of those experiences of judgment, and I don't discourage judgment. In fact, today I tell leaders and teams I coach to let their judgment stimulate their wonder.

Judgment is often conflated with the state of being judgmental and all the negative connotations that holds. Judgment itself is not negative. Consider the definition: judgment is "the ability to form valuable opinions and make good decisions."[1] What's wrong with that? Nothing. The confusion surrounding judgment versus judgmental has encouraged us, at least in the West, to suspend *all* judgment. By encouraging people to embrace judgment, I simply want them to restore their appreciation for discernment.

It's OK to allow a reaction to arise when an event occurs. Instead of squashing down that initial reaction in fear of being judgmental, what might happen if people stepped into judgment and generated "good decisions"? If we can pay attention when judgment shows up

---

1   *Cambridge Advanced Learner's Dictionary*, 4th ed. (Cambridge: Cambridge University Press, 2013), s.v. "Judgment," https://dictionary.cambridge.org/dictionary/english/judgment.

and stay with it just a little bit longer, it gives us the opportunity to let curiosity bubble—curiosity that can lead to a state of wonder.

Modern assumptions about the word "wonder" can cause confusion about what I mean here. The etymology of the term can help—consider the Old English *wundrian* "be astonished" or "admire; make wonderful, magnify."[2] When I ask leaders to let their judgment stimulate *wonder*, I'm referring to that rapt state of attentiveness and astonishment at something new and mysterious to what they (think) they already know.

Stimulating wonder through judgment often starts with questioning the judgmental voice. Tackling judgment can be as simple as saying, in a personal context, "I wonder what's happening for this person? Why are they acting this way?" or, in a professional context, "I wonder what we missed with this data? What bias was operating when we gathered and analyzed it?" These examples show how, by questioning judgment, we can start to depersonalize the issue. We remove ourselves from the equation and examine the situation with a big-picture and systemic lens.

When we depersonalize, we're regaining control. We've got our hands on the steering wheel, and we're looking down the road and seeing not just the red light in front of us but also the road beyond, leading to the horizon. And we wonder: *What's on that horizon? How do we get there?* And then we open ourselves up to new ways of getting there. That's why I tell my coaching clients to tap into their judgments, examine them carefully, and let them lead the way to wonder.

---

2   *Online Etymology Dictionary*, 2023 ed. (Douglas Harper), s.v. "Wonder," https://www.etymonline.com/word/wonder.

The Foundational Role of Fear in My Coaching Career

Overcoming fear and allowing judgment to inspire wonder are two pillars that make up the crux of my coaching. This is something I came to realize even before I identified as a "coach"—at a time before "coaching" was really a thing.

Before I became a coach, I spent fourteen years working at Charles Schwab. I'd tried all kinds of things before that. After breaking off my first run at college—pre-med at the University of California (UC), Santa Barbara—in favor of a European adventure (more to come on *that*), I returned to San Francisco and worked in the garment division of General Mills. That was the fall of 1979.

I was about three years in when I thought, *You know what? This isn't for me*, and quit. After that, I worked six part-time jobs to make ends meet: I counted inventory at a manufacturing firm in Silicon Valley, I wrote term papers, I reupholstered furniture, I did some catering gigs, I tailored clothes, and I had that illustrious cold-calling gig at Shearson Lehman that I mentioned.

I also went back to school at San Francisco State and ended up graduating cum laude with a degree in economics and finance. This was in the fall of 1982, and the US was in a recession—meaning there were no jobs to be had for a young grad like me. What to do? My mother told me, "You'll never starve if you learn how to type." She was right.

I went to Manpower to find a job, and, following the typing test, they sent me to work at the US Regional Post Office. I was typing for nine gentlemen who would write out their letters to people in long hand on yellow legal pads. Then I'd type those letters up with a word processor, print them, and mail them out. It wasn't a stimulating job, but it paid the bills—and since I didn't have funds left over to print cover letters and résumés, they gave me permission to stay late and use the office equipment.

I was scouring job ads when I saw this three-line print ad in the *San Francisco Chronicle* for Schwab. They were looking for candidates for a management trainee program on the West Coast. I landed a spot and got my first job before the six-month program was over. It was a pivotal moment in my career, as I stayed at Schwab until 1996.

In that time, I worked in almost every single division of the organization. For my final assignment, I was put in charge of an initiative redesigning the Schwab customer experience. We had just gone public, and Chuck—as everyone called Charles Schwab in the office—had decided it was time to change the branch offices into sales offices. The project was a hot potato that nobody wanted—except for me. I just thought, *That sounds like a grand adventure.*

Talking to my teammates, I identified two major challenges. First, we had to level the power dynamics between the executives and the branch office receptionists and customer service agents. The branch office personnel were on the front lines; they heard the voice of the customer every single day. The executives had to be able to have a conversation with those colleagues about how to redesign the customer experience and not get caught up in, "I know better than you"—because they didn't. They didn't live the day-to-day experience of the customer like the branch office receptionists and customer service agents did.

The other challenge we had to overcome was fear that drove resistance to change. I told my team, "We have to face the fear that people are going to have that they can't learn to sell successfully. They came to this organization *because* they didn't have to sell." That was one of the key things about discount brokerage.

Ultimately, the process we used became what would be called "team coaching" today. It required starting with an inquiry process, seeing beyond the situation, activating imagination, and accepting the brainstorming principle that all ideas are good ideas. Then, we grounded our thinking with continuous experimentation and assessed the outcomes—all the while learning to listen and suspend bias, assumptions, and preferences. It was my first "coaching" experience, not that I would have labeled it as such.

That "grand adventure" was a grand success. We got the project done under budget and on time, and we met the workforce retention goal. And I realized that I'd found what I was supposed to be doing, which is helping people level the playing field around power dynamics and face things that feel scary with optimism and confidence. That's basically shorthand for "coaching" with groups and teams.

An exclamation point for that moment of realization came in the form of a white suit. I was preparing to present the new customer experience design we'd developed. It was the morning of my presentation. We were convening the first two hundred senior leaders to hear about the new customer experience design—and I spilled a cup of coffee down the front of my dress two hours before we were supposed to start.

> **I realized that I'd found what I was supposed to be doing, which is helping people level the playing field around power dynamics and face things that feel scary with optimism and confidence.**

One of our consultants shrugged and said, "Come on, let's go to Neiman Marcus." We did, and I bought this gorgeous white suit. Normally, I was a plain dresser. It had never been my approach to impress through appearances. But that suit looked like a million bucks.

Shortly after, there I was, on a raised platform, in my white suit, in front of two hundred people, introducing "Welcome Rep," the new customer experience program. The reaction was one I'll never forget. Not only did people clap and cheer, but they also stood up. We hadn't even implemented the program yet. I was only introducing the pilot. But that reaction was stunning to me. It was the first time I had done something that had really come from within me, had invited others to collaborate, and had solved a problem in a big way for people who appreciated that solution.

Leveraging Judgment and Fear to Stimulate Wonder

Back at Schwab, I didn't identify as a coach. It's only in retrospect that I see what I was doing was coaching people. Now, decades later, I'm still coaching people. Over my coaching career, I've worked with leaders, teams, and enterprises across six continents. I know something about workplace climate and how leaders influence it. All the people I've worked with share one desire: to be their best selves and, as part of that, live their best lives—to realize their bliss.

See, fear has this wonderful counterpoint: bliss, those sparkling moments of ecstasy that sit in your memory like carefully guarded gems. How do you know you're having a moment of bliss? This is a question I broach frequently in my coaching because it's a core value of my organization, inviteCHANGE—and I think it's something that people often dismiss as unattainable, which I don't believe.

I think recognizing bliss requires quieting our cognition enough to pay attention to our sensory experiences. Not enough people get an opportunity for that. They usually have their senses assaulted by horns and machinery and urban life. Conversely, some people feel assaulted by silence; they have difficulty sitting in quietness. There's an entire sleep industry hawking white noise machines for exactly this reason. Bliss can be elusive—but that's exactly what this book is striving for.

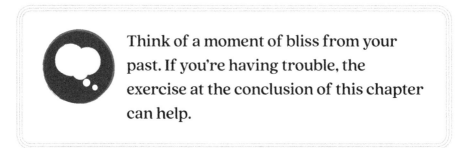

Think of a moment of bliss from your past. If you're having trouble, the exercise at the conclusion of this chapter can help.

Here's one of my moments of bliss: It dates to my sophomore year of high school, when I participated in a five-day orienteering experience in southern Missouri. We learned to read a map and use a compass. Then, we went out to spend a day in the wilderness alone. The Midwest is pretty flat, but I found a hillside to climb. At the top, I sat on a ledge and dangled my legs over as I looked down at a river in the valley below. I pulled a grapefruit out of my backpack, took my Swiss Army knife out, cut the grapefruit open, and sat and ate while watching that dazzling river.

To this day, I have never had a better tasting grapefruit. The sun was shining; I could hear the water and the birds; I was eating this amazing piece of fruit. That was bliss. And part of that bliss was knowing that I'd found my own way to the top of that hill.

It's a beautiful metaphor for how I've lived my life since then. No matter what's happened, I've always trusted that I could find my way. However, it took that moment of stopping and sitting still for me to realize that. If I'd just kept on moving up the hillside, I might have missed that moment of bliss.

That's what I'm asking you to do: sit still. It's been suggested that human knowledge is doubling every twelve hours. With artificial intelligence (AI), that could become every twelve seconds. In a world that's speeding up, it's more critical than ever to slow down, reflect, and move forward judiciously, contemplatively, and with respect for your personal wholeness and the wholeness of those around you.

Slowing Down and Tolerating Tension

With this book, I'm asking you to pause. I'm asking you to sit in all the tension of the moment and all the ugly sentiments—judgment, doubt, self-critique, fear—of that tension. The question is, how does someone learn to tolerate the tension of presence? You must build on the known while also trusting the unknown.

My organization has done extensive research into tension in the workplace. The following table introduces a set of everyday tensions that our research with over 250 leaders revealed. A look at one of these tensions can help illustrate the value of slowing down.

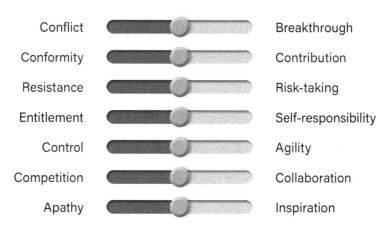

SEVEN COMMON LEADER DILEMMAS

Conflict	Breakthrough
Conformity	Contribution
Resistance	Risk-taking
Entitlement	Self-responsibility
Control	Agility
Competition	Collaboration
Apathy	Inspiration

Consider breakthrough and conflict. Sometimes, conflict is healthy. If you tolerate the tension of conflict for a little bit longer, it becomes a way to foster freedom, turning what appears to be damaging into a more desirable state—like a breakthrough idea rather than the breakdown of paralyzing conflict. However, if you go to break through too quickly, without reflecting on what breakdown contributes, you might do something impulsive, reckless, or damaging.

I know you're skeptical that slowing down is the answer. Of course, you are. Because all you hear in your professional life is go faster and do more with less. Thousands of book titles are providing you guidance about how to do exactly that—to be more productive, effective, organized, and so on. It's exhausting.

And I know you're tired. Maybe you're not sleeping enough or eating well. Maybe you overindulge in your vice of choice. Yet, you keep doing it because it helps you cope with the intensity of everyday life. No shame, no blame. It's not your fault. You're living in a system that rewards you for doing that. But it's probably not going to lead to any kind of bliss.

Speeding ahead without sitting in the presence of tension isn't going to get you the results you want as a leader—for yourself, for your teams, or for your organization. When you're able to slow down and reflect, you can better tap into the potential you hold and that your teams and your organization hold. You can identify resources, tangible and intangible, to be deployed—and you can innovate, developing creative solutions for problems you might otherwise have steamrolled over on your mission to keep racing ahead.

What's more, by allowing yourself, as a leader, to personally connect with the possibilities of tolerating tension, you are allowing your workforce to connect with those possibilities as well. This can help create a safer, more inclusive space, where workers feel seen and valued—not hustled along. This is something great leaders can't discount, notably in light of shifting workforce demands and growing struggles to retain talent.

Many organizations are navigating this stony path now. Gartner uses the term "The Human Deal" to speak to shifting workforce demands. Workers are seeking more value from work beyond paychecks alone.[3] According to Gartner's research, employees want five "human" components: deeper connections, radical flexibility, personal growth, holistic well-being, and shared purpose. Those are all things that speak to elements of humanity—like the simple desire for a calm moment of bliss—that are often overlooked by corporate agendas.

Coaching is all about improving performance and producing desirable and sustainable results. However, for decades, we've been operating under the delusion that the best results come from being the fastest, biggest, greatest—pick whatever superlative you like. The tide is turning. We are seeing employees needing more *humanity* at work.

How is your organization meeting that need? As a leader, what are you doing to heed that call? What are the consequences of ignoring that call? Conversely, where might you and your organization end up if you learn to tolerate the presence of tension—and leverage that tension to embrace the judgment and wonder that all people hold within them?

Generative change is the vehicle I propose to get you there. That's what this book is all about.

---

3   Jordan Turner, "Employees Seek Personal Value and Purpose at Work. Be Prepared to Deliver," *Gartner*, March 29, 2023, https://www.gartner.com/en/articles/ employees-seek-personal-value-and-purpose-at-work-be-prepared-to-deliver.

EXERCISE: IDENTIFY YOUR BLISS

Coaching is overtly focused on improving leadership, communication, and performance. The unspoken and oft-ignored goal of coaching is simply this: bliss. Before engaging with the coaching process, it's helpful to identify your own moment of bliss. If you're having trouble identifying yours, the HeartMath Institute has a simple heart coherence meditation that can help.[4] It takes only about five minutes. I've adapted it here.

1. Start by doing some breathing. Shift your attention to your body. Focus on your big toe. Wiggle it. Focus on your stomach. Relax it. Now, focus on your chest and your breathing.

2. Sit in the moment. Breathe in and out, imagining the air going in and out of your lungs. As you do so, think back to a memory that gives you a positive feeling.

3. Try to reexperience that good feeling—that moment of bliss. Focus on that feeling as you continue to breathe in and out, fixating on all the elements that made up that moment: sights, sounds, smells.

4. Keep breathing in that memory until you're back *in* the memory, living it viscerally again.

5. Express gratitude for that memory before bringing your attention back into the room, returning to the current time and space.

---

4   HeartMath Institute, "The Quick Coherence® Technique for Adults," accessed August 15, 2023, https://www.heartmath.org/resources/heartmath-tools/quick-coherence-technique-for-adults/.

6. If you enjoy writing in a journal, now is a good time to grab it and notice any personal insights about how that memory of bliss shapes who you are today.

STEP 5: EXPRESS GRATITUDE.

STEP 4: KEEP BREATHING.

STEP 3: REEXPERIENCE THE FEELING.

STEP 2: SIT IN THE MOMENT.

STEP 1: BREATHE.

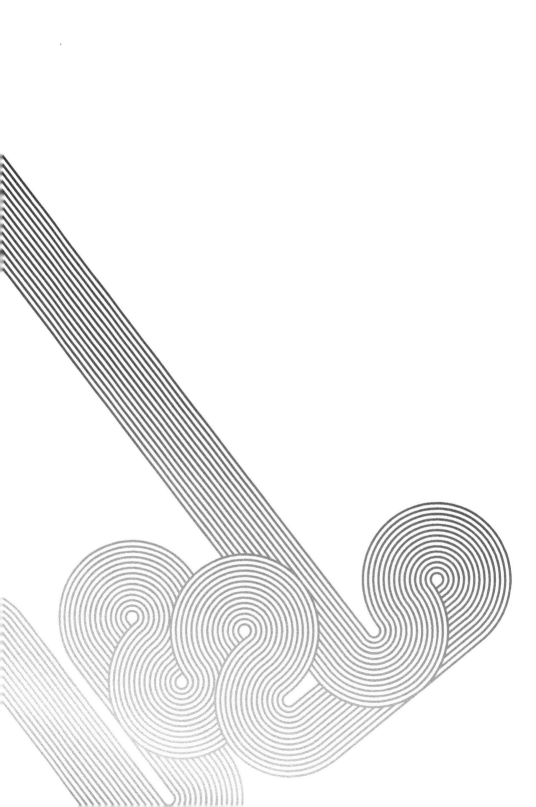

CHAPTER 1

MAKE IT YOURS

*Learn to use your brain power. Critical thinking is
the key to creative problem solving in business.*
—RICHARD BRANSON, BUSINESS MAGNATE

I've always stood out from the crowd. Born with a port-wine mark on my face, there was no point trying to blend in, and I became independent at a young age as a result. My family situation contributed: I grew up with three older brothers, and both of my parents worked. There was no coddling at home. I took up sports to try to fit in but only ended up sticking out more through my athletic career. I became a competitive swimmer at four and a competitive figure skater at six.

I went on to coach figure skating in college while studying pre-med at the University of California (UC), Santa Barbara. But I didn't enjoy it—the coaching (ironically) or the college experience. UC Santa Barbara was full of partiers back then, and that wasn't my scene. I decided it wasn't for me and ran off on a European adventure.

You could say my entire life has been a pursuit of grand adventures; this was one of the earliest ones I embarked on.

I was nineteen when I left college—my parents weren't very happy about this—and went to visit a family friend in Sweden. I got my passport and planned my wardrobe. In those days, one of the things I did for fun was to design and sew clothes. So, I had sewn a lot of my wardrobe, and I had this one outfit I was particularly proud of: a styling white fedora with a black band, long palazzo-style pants, and a bustier top.

I was so naïve that I spent more time planning my outfits than the trip itself. When I landed in Gothenburg, I found I hadn't translated the time difference correctly—and I was a day early. The family friend who was supposed to pick me up at the airport wasn't there, and I couldn't get ahold of her. Keep in mind, this was an era before cell phones.

What now? I didn't speak a word of Swedish. I found an airport locker for my luggage and grabbed my little backpack and figured out how to take a bus to the city. From there, I figured I'd take the train to the family friend's home—I knew the address, thankfully. But the train didn't leave for a few hours.

No problem. I'd do some exploring. I left the train station and started wandering the streets of Gothenburg, soaking it up. Then I noticed somebody following me. At first, I wasn't sure, because it started with that hair-raising feeling—that tingle at the nape of the neck, a warning sign that somebody was watching. It was my body telling me what my brain hadn't yet realized: *danger!*

I'd stop every now and then to look over my shoulder, and I'd still see this guy, and I realized he was definitely following me. For a moment, I panicked. Then, I came up with a plan: I'd walk into the nearest department store and head straight to the women's lingerie department.

So that's what I did. I made a beeline for it and just grabbed something off the rack and went into a changing room. I hung out in there for about twenty minutes. When I came back out, I didn't see the guy who'd been following me. Once I was sure he was gone, I left via a different exit than the one I'd come in. I managed to connect with the family friend shortly after.

That was a grand adventure that could have taken an ugly turn. I still give myself a lot of credit for not completely collapsing into a puddle of tears, given how young and naïve I was. I listened to my body; I didn't ignore that creepy-crawly feeling at the back of my neck; once I confirmed that I was indeed being followed, I acted.

That's exactly how I hope you'll approach this book—by listening to your body and following your intuition.

How to Make This Book Relevant to You

This isn't a book that you have to read from cover to cover. Instead, I encourage you to identify the topics you want to engage with according to your gut instinct—according to what sparks emotion in you, be it judgment, fear, curiosity, wonder. I want you to create your own grand adventure with this book. You can check the table of contents, pick a topic that excites you or speaks to what you are going through in some part of your life, and skip right to it.

And I don't want you to just *read*. I want you to engage with this book proactively and *make it yours*. To read in a relevant way, consider what's happening for you in your professional role, family life, or community. Think about where you've found yourself stuck, frustrated, disappointed, angry, or afraid—and not sure whether to fight, flee, freeze, or fracture.

As you read, pay attention to your visceral bodily reactions. Take a moment to quiet your conscious thoughts, and give way to the physical. Is there a section that gives you goosebumps? Dog-ear the page. Is there a sentence that makes you instinctively shudder with unwelcome self-recognition? Highlight it. Is there an entire topic you're tempted to skip because it seems too sticky? I'm going to let you in on a secret: that might be the topic that you'll most benefit from.

At the same time, pay attention to your body. As you capture the details of a story, notice if your body gets tight or relaxed—whether you're experiencing annoyance or delight. Browse a few pages, and let them activate your own memories and emotions. By engaging with the book in this way, you'll make it relevant to you. You'll also start to slow down.

When is the last time you fully slowed down and relaxed—like you could almost physically feel your body exhale its tension? Maybe you were getting a massage or coming home from a long trip. Tap into that moment now. Remember that energy and how it physically affected you.

Those moments of slowing down are sort of like whitewater rafting. If you've ever done it, you're familiar with the stillness that comes before you go over a big drop in elevation. There are a lot of rocks, and the water is running fast beneath, but you're lulled into a kind of complacency because the surface looks calm. Right around the corner is the raging water, and you're not sure you're ready for it. What's your response?

For some people, the response is adrenaline. For other people, the response is terror. In either case, the emotional response is going to hijack the full functioning of the brain. Human neurobiology, by design, brings attention to threats—like when the man was following me in Gothenburg, or when you're getting ready to go down a raging rapid. The body releases chemicals so that the brain focuses on these possible threats.

As a result, we don't always accurately assess the danger. We worry we don't have what it takes to rise to it. The truth is, we always have what it takes to rise to it, and we're going to rise to it more effectively if we can relax the parasympathetic system and articulate to ourselves, *I've got this. I'm whole, resourceful, capable, and creative.* In the case of a raging rapid, that thought might be, *I'm familiar with this challenge. I'm in good physical condition. I have great teammates in the boat with me.*

In the case of my Gothenburg experience, it was about reminding myself, *I'm not alone. There are safe spaces. There are people to help. I am smart and independent and can navigate myself to a place where I feel secure, even in a foreign country.*

However, when we face such threatening moments, we're often hijacked by emotionality, and a threat we *can* handle becomes a threat we think we *can't* handle. This is because we aren't using our full mental capacity. Everything becomes focused on the physical, biological reaction of flight, fight, freeze, or fracture. The body is stimulated through a release of hormones, and we might feel shortness of breath or tightness in our shoulders or a scary pit in the stomach—all physical attributes pointing to the beginning of the emotional hijack.

If we can identify that moment and recognize it for what it is, we can short-circuit it. We can self-regulate our emotions and quiet the parasympathetic system. Cultural anthropologist Angeles Arrien declared that medium-slow is nature's rhythm, while the Western rhythm is fast-overdrive. Slowing down is an obvious opportunity to live activated from our authentic self.

Studies of the brain show that, when we feel over-activated and want to move to a more balanced state, the simple act of a deep sigh, followed by a deep inhale and a slow turn of the neck, adjusts our nervous system enough to move out of a reactive posture of fright, flight, freeze, or fracture.[5] A mindfulness or contemplative practice reminds us that all things are possible in the stillness of a quiet mind.

Similarly, in our experiences with others, allowing moments of pause infused with full presence evokes deeper inquiry, surprise, and revelation, in any domain of life. It all starts with realizing that taking a pause creates more time than it takes.

When you engage with the generative vehicle for change, you'll start to recognize the adrenaline rush of terror when it occurs—and to logically argue with it. It's not about eliminating the emotional side, because it's a protective instinct you need to survive, but about questioning it. Ask yourself, *What's true here? Is the fear real? Is the fear real, relative to who I know myself to be?* When you do that, you're telling your brain, "I'm in control. Let's use our logic and sort out what makes sense to do here."

> **Taking a pause creates more time than it takes.**

---

5   Jan-Marino Ramirez, "The Integrative Role of the Sigh in Psychology, Physiology, Pathology, and Neurobiology," *Progress in Brain Research* 209 (2014): 91–129, https://doi.org/10.1016/B978-0-444-63274-6.00006-0.

As a process flow, being first with the body, then the heart, and last the head. Not the other way around. And that's how I want you to read this book: body, heart, head. That's how you'll make it uniquely yours and indisputably relevant to you. However, to make it *meaningful* to you, you have to take the next step: reflection.

From Relevant Reading to Reflection

Make this book relevant to you, and, in the process, let it inspire reflection. I think that's the most important mindset you can have when approaching this book. Reflection is the key that unlocks the door to valuable perspectives, answers, and solutions because you start to realize, *There's a pattern here. Every time I see this scenario, I react like this. Why am I doing that?* Being curious about your motivation for thoughts and actions provides the first step to changing habits. But you don't get to that moment of internal curiosity without the act of reflecting.

Reflection is often treated as a passive process when, in fact, reflection is active. It requires training. A lot of this book is about strengthening your reflection muscle. My hope is that by the time you finish reading it, reflection will become your new habit. It will become your trusted advisor—your answer to any thorny problem you face.

Let's say you're going through this book, and you have a moment of recognition. Something sparks a reaction in you. Let's say an example raises a memory of a similar experience you've had yourself. How do you move from that visceral reaction, recognizing the relevance to yourself, to reflection—in an active, productive, meaningful way? What are the practices that allow you to pause outer life for a moment? During the pause moment—yes, moment not hours—you can question yourself internally. Bring your focus to what motivates your perception of that remembered experience and how you make meaning of it.

This requires pressing pause and asking yourself questions. Reflection is often asking: *What happened here? What's important here? What did I desire here? How clear was I about what I desired? Did I just go into it completely tabula rasa and then wonder why things happened the way they did?*

Reflection is a micro-skill that's grossly misunderstood. Leaders shy away from it, thinking it will cost them time. But pause creates more time than it takes, because pause allows you to access your inner wisdom and experiential knowledge—your own physical sense of instinct and intuition and emotional sense of fit and alignment. In the normal hustle of daily life, those things aren't easily accessible to you.

One way to frame your reflection process is to write an intention statement. Writing intention statements becomes a deliberate technique to focus your felt sensations and emotions. A sensory declaration operates similarly to the way a musical instrument is tuned for a certain key and pitch. The instruments you are tuning include your body and your heart. Through intention statements, you deliberately signal to the body and heart what you choose to experience in a given situation.

QUICK ACTIVITY: PRACTICE WRITING AN INTENTION STATEMENT

Intention statements can help us exercise our reflection muscle. An intention statement is spoken in the first-person voice, in the present tense, using language that is both sensory and emotional. This rubric can help you practice your intention statements, driving reflection as you approach the topics to come.

Intention Statement

A written statement declaring the felt and sensed experience you desire.

Expressed in the "I" personal voice with present tense verbs.

Example:
I practice harmonious pause, noticing opportunities for change

FELT AND SENSED WORDS		
Excited	Gratified	Overjoyed
Confident	Determined	Spirited
Elated	Fearless	Worthy
Bold	Exhilarated	Passionate
Daring	Energized	Secure

Say you want to improve your physical fitness. A simple intention statement to motivate fitness could be this, "I experience vitality and stamina during daily exercise." Through this statement, you realize that, although the circumstances of your fitness may not change immediately, how you relate to those circumstances can shift in a second. Change, at least in the mind, can be truly instantaneous. This becomes especially true and more powerful as you become more adept at claiming your sovereignty.

> **Change, at least in the mind, can be truly instantaneous.**

(Re)claiming Your Sovereignty

Sovereignty is the path to leading well. The term has evolved beyond the geopolitical sphere and is now commonly used in human development and leadership circles. I define it as follows:

Sovereignty is the quality of accepting responsibility for our inner authority to choose how we relate with the circumstances of our own lives. When we take our life into our own hands, we also take upon our self to act with integrity and gain response-agility with our life, our family, our community, our fellow human beings, and the planet as a whole.

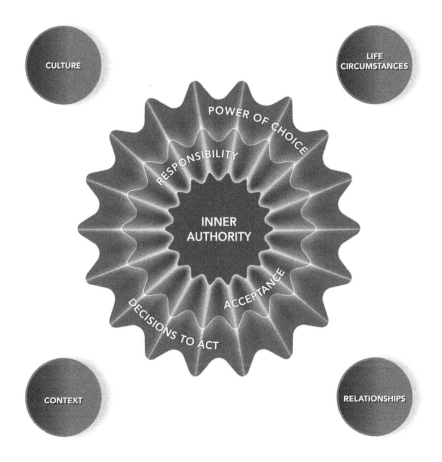

An underpinning of being in the world from a state of Generative Wholeness™—which I discuss in the second chapter—is recognizing your own sovereignty, your responsibility to your inner authority. It's your responsibility to choose how you relate to the conditions of your life. Viktor E. Frankl famously said, "[U]ntil his last breath no one can wrest from a man his freedom to take one or another attitude toward his destiny."[6] That's an extreme way of putting it, but the idea holds: when you relinquish your power to something outside of yourself, you lose your ability to shape your self-identity and, with it, your destiny.

---

6   Viktor E. Frankel, *Man's Search for Meaning: An Introduction to Logotherapy* (Boston: Beacon Press, 1962).

This also speaks to the concept of accountability, a frequently misunderstood and abused phrase these days. People often talk about *holding others accountable*, but this is, in my view, a myth. Only you can hold yourself accountable. My five-word definition of accountability is accepting responsibility for authority granted. Someone may grant you authority—say, a boss may entrust you with a project—but *you* are the one who is *accepting* that responsibility. You are always in the driver's seat.

This brings me back to sovereignty—*the quality of accepting responsibility for our inner authority to choose how we relate with the circumstances of our own lives.* Sovereignty is, first, an internal process—accepting the idea that you get to author your life. Beyond that, it's a relational process—what are the agreements you have with others about your mutual expectations or conditions of satisfaction?

Again, the obvious example is your boss assigning you a project. Everything in life is a request and a promise, and this is no exception. Your boss, the requestor, delegates the assignment. You, the promiser, accept responsibility for that delegation. However, the way the requestor and the promiser interpret that delegation may be different—because they are two distinct individuals. Each person is operating from their own context, both past and present, which will impact how they interpret the ask.

Most organizations get in trouble when the conversation stops. The requestor makes a request, the promiser says OK, and they don't dive deeper. They're too busy. The promiser doesn't say, "Let's make sure that we're translating this the same way." The longer the requestor and the promiser can stay in dialogue and flesh out the conditions of satisfaction, the greater the likelihood of a satisfactory outcome for both sides. Sovereignty is what allows that conversation to happen.

Sovereignty is also what allows people to see beyond and push against the systems designed to keep them stagnant and attached to the status quo. Institutional systems reinforce that change is hard and takes a long time. Humans live inside of systems, most of them implemented decades if not centuries ago, and don't even recognize them or remember why those systems were implemented as they were.

Take the education system. There's this idea that kids need to go to school for twelve years and that they need to focus on the core curriculum of reading, writing, and science, technology, engineering, and mathematics (STEM). But not all kids need a full twelve years. Not all kids learn well through traditional models. Neurodivergent individuals may benefit from so-called compassionate pedagogies, for instance.[7] There are Montessori or Waldorf schools that focus on sensory experiences and emotional systems. But the overarching model, the public school system—the literal institution of education in the US—is still very rote. The US still uses standardized tests as a measure of a child's ability.

This opens a whole other conversation into how institutional systems are designed to discriminate and repress. Systemic racism is nurtured by institutional "norms" that are only in recent years beginning to be questioned widely. These institutional systems are everywhere. There is blatant disregard for humanity all over the world, from the way people of color are treated in America to the way the Rohingya are treated in China or the way slaves—literal slaves—are exploited in the diamond mines of certain African countries. The issues of Diversity, Equity, Inclusion, Justice, and Belonging (DEIJB) are ubiquitous in the human family.

DEIJB has become its own methodology, pedagogy, and set of theories in reaction to those systems. At the macro level, the thing

---

7   Lorna G. Hamilton and Stephanie Petty, "Compassionate Pedagogy for Neurodiversity in Higher Education: A Conceptual Analysis," *Frontiers in Psychology* 14 (2023): 1093290, https://doi.org/10.3389/fpsyg.2023.1093290.

all people have in common is their humanity. When we accept our common humanity, we can celebrate diversity in the human family. However, we get attached to our difference, and we have a need to be evaluative about that difference. This creates a series of ripple effects, including institutional systems that hold racism, caste systems, and other schemes of difference in place.

There are also patriarchal systems. I've had plenty of experiences with the misogyny they perpetuate. When I worked for General Mills in San Francisco, I was sent to New York for an annual sales meeting. I was nineteen at the time, and I was the only female in the room with a bunch of old white-haired men who were the most misogynistic I'd ever witnessed—raunchy jokes, pats on the head, calling me "little girl." This was 1978.

The California office I was representing had sold the most goods of any of the other offices around the country. Was that acknowledged? No. Who was running that office? Me, the "little girl." It became clear to me that the system dictated that who you knew and who you hung out with during off hours was far more important than the reality of results being produced. Very early on, I got that the world was not wired for acknowledging results.

Back then, my reaction was "Screw you." Today, that's still my reaction—but I also approach the situation with more thoughtfulness. Because I wonder, how do we create misogynists? What makes men (and sometimes women) feel better about themselves when they diminish the feminine? I've found that often men actually want more access to their own feminine.

Again, these are fairly new conversations. Only in recent years have we been telling young boys, "Hey, it's OK to share your feelings, to cry"—actions associated more with the feminine than the masculine—because for years, we've told boys it's *not* OK to access these feminine elements.

This book does not explicitly address how organizations and leaders can be effective in transforming their systems—that would require an entire other book (and I'm not a DEIJB expert). However, this book will support you in transforming your *internal* system—those personal habits, preferences, assumptions, and biases—that are creating tension for you and standing in the way of your ability to recognize the commonality of the human family while also celebrating the differences within it.

Systems like these—patriarchal, racist—are designed to squash your sovereignty. They also make change seem hard. There are systemic reasons for that. The narratives of "change is hard" or "change takes a long time" are man-made. For proof of the alternative, just look to nature. Take the seasons. It only takes three months, and suddenly, you are in a whole new relationship to planet Earth. Still, you ignore the evidence that change happens in an instant in favor of something external—a system that's holding you in place, ascribing value to what's comfortable and familiar, otherwise known as the status quo.

The status quo isn't going to reward your sovereignty. It's up to *you* to seize your sovereignty and take your life in your own hands. And once you do that, once you are comfortable leading yourself, you will be ready to tap into a new superpower—fearless intuition.

When is the last time you challenged the status quo? Have you ever? What is a component of the status quo—in your personal or work life, or more broadly socially—you want to challenge?

Learning to Exercise Your Fearless Use of Intuition

Asking people what their superpower is seems to be a question *du jour*, thus one I get asked with surprising frequency. By now, I've got my answer down: my superpower is fearless intuition. Sometimes my intuition tells me things and my response is, "Really? You sure?" I question my intuition. But I also trust it.

My fearless intuition developed early, out of need. As a kid who was "different," despite what my parents tried to tell me, I had to develop a strong sixth sense to determine if a situation or a person was safe or not. This need was also the result of my extreme independence and my pursuit of an athletic career at such a young age. I was out in the world doing my own thing. And while I saw the world as a grand adventure, not something to be afraid of, I also learned to listen to my intuition fearlessly, just like I did that day in Gothenburg.

From my experience, the breakthrough in self-trust, and sovereignty is sourced from fearless use of intuition. This is a core element of a generative leader. However, there are many people who won't listen to their intuition at all. If they can't make sense of something in an evidence-based way, they're not interested. They want the comfort of what they can tangibly *know*.

How do you push outside of your comfort zone, that innate desire to trust only what's tangible, and learn to trust in the unknown, the intangible? The way you approach this book is a first step. It starts with realizing where you're coming from and acknowledging that you're going to be reading through that lens. If you're a CEO, you'll read this book differently than if you were, say, a not-for-profit board director or an educator. A parent will read this book differently from a nonparent. A self-employed individual will read this book differently from an employee.

Next, recognize what you don't know. If you're operating out of status quo or habits or preferences, then you must be, by definition, pushing something aside. You're cutting off access to the full picture of what's going on. Acknowledge what you don't know about life, leading, society, humanity, organizations, and systems. If you're really honest with yourself, that's likely a lengthy list.

This will allow you to reconstruct a new way of experiencing and to being impacted and influenced by others in ways that feel foreign to you. Expect some discomfort—or even fear. But as that fear dissipates, you'll be able to listen more carefully *internally*. Then, finally, you can say, "Based on what I know, I can face the uncertainty because I trust myself to rise and meet whatever shows up in front of me."

I trust that you may be skeptical. But the process itself isn't complicated, once you break it down into those steps:

- Notice and realize your context. What are you paying attention to? What motivates you to take that point of view?

- Recognize what you don't know consciously, and what you therefore choose to pursue unconsciously.

- Reconstruct a new way of experiencing.

You can use this book and how you approach it as a practice run of sorts. In the case of this book, that new way of experiencing might translate to a new way of reading—we might call it reading relevantly.

This is not a book to read before you go to bed. And it's not a book to sit down and read from cover to cover. It is a book to luxuriate with. This book may make your head hurt, just like my coaching methods sometimes make my clients' heads hurt. Think of those twinges as a sign that your various muscles—your reflection, your intuition—are flexing and growing. When you build those muscles, some soreness is inevitable. If you're feeling overwhelmed, put the book down and take a break. Talk to a friend about what troubles you. Compare notes with a colleague. Great leaders seek external input all the time. They aren't leading in a vacuum.

When I work with clients, I often ask them as we start a session, "How are you showing up today?" And clients may say, "Oh my God, I just came out of the worst meeting ever." That's when I tell them, "OK, why don't you stand up for a second and just take a few deep breaths? Let yourself release the meeting and get present with our time together here." And we just stay quiet and self-regulate. When the client sits back down, there's often a noticeable shift—a softening in the face or a dropping of the hunched shoulders. The posture becomes less defensive, as we create a climate that feels safe.

That is how I hope you will show up to this book. Take a deep breath and relax. And then be prepared to work—to make it relevant, to reflect, to step into your sovereignty. And, above all, be prepared to entertain your sense of wonder. Think of it like laying on your back and looking up at the stars in the sky. That's a state of wonder.

When we embrace that kind of expansiveness, it becomes easier to see what we've ignored, dismissed, or deflected in the past—and to change. It gets easier to admit, "The way I am making choices about what actions to pursue is not producing the result I want. If I really want to sustain excellence, I've got to change my rubric." The rubric I'm proposing to you, and that I hope you'll entertain, is Generative Wholeness™.

EXERCISE: RECOGNIZE YOUR LENS

(Re)claiming your sovereignty requires a fearless use of intuition. The way you approach this book is a first step to deliberately using intuition on your own behalf. In fact, you can use this book as a practice exercise to tune yourself just as you would an instrument. If this book is going to help you reconstruct a new way of thinking about, experiencing, and interacting with the world, you've got to start by realizing what's influencing how you understand your current state. Start by answering these questions.

1. Professionally, what stage am I in, for example, early career, mid-career, in succession pipeline, and so on?

2. What's my next step of development as a leader?

3. What do I already know and claim as wisdom and expertise through my experiences?

Jot down those answers. Keep in mind: This is the lens you will read through, inherently. My aim is to get you to pause, reflect, and question that lens. Now, recognize what you don't yet know by answering these questions:

4. What leadership setback haunts me?

5. What more do I want to learn—about leading, organizations, humanity, society?

6. What gaps in my development cause me to feel self-conscious?

Jot down those answers (recognizing that this list isn't exhaustive). By acknowledging what you don't know, you're opening the door to wonder—and to reconstructing.

Keep your answers to these questions on hand as you make your way through this book. Remind yourself what you do and don't know. This will allow you to "read relevantly" and make this text significant to you and your unique experience as a human.

CHAPTER 2

GENERATIVE WHOLENESS™

Only when you've first developed clarity, courage, and commitment will you know how to exert the leverage to really make a difference.
—DAN MILLMAN, SPEAKER, AND AUTHOR
OF *THE LIFE YOU WERE BORN TO LIVE*

Everything I'm presenting to you in this book has come out of my work with clients. I'm doing the best I can to dissolve the mystery that surrounds coaching and why coaching works. My experience covers a wide swath of individuals. I've worked with people from their late twenties to their seventies and collaborated with everyone from executive leaders to middle management. I've coached people with MBAs, those who haven't graduated high school, and everyone in between.

In all that work, I've found that tensions of presence usually arise because people don't live in a state of wholeness. They neglect their essence—that is, the core or true self, stripped of the convenience of personality—and instead cling to a constructed persona. In the introduction to this book, I mentioned that most of the leaders I've worked with adopt an expected identity, both to achieve and to avoid feeling uncomfortable. The problem with clinging to that identity is that it often ignores the essence and, in doing so, denies the possibility of true sovereignty and the bliss a person experiences through a sovereign mindset.

Sovereignty, a responsibility we access to listen to our inner authority, empowers us to choose how we relate to the conditions of our life. When we give away our power to something external, we lose our ability to shape our essence's expression and our self-identity and, with it, to control our path forward. Yet it's such a common problem: Why don't we have fluidity to operate from the authentic self and to exercise sovereignty in our daily lives? Why is it so hard?

Pause. Do you feel that you allow your essence, your true self, to come through in life? At work? At home? With friends? With your partner? With coworkers? Why or why not?

I've seen my clients grapple with this hurdle on many occasions. One comes to mind in particular; I'll call him Ricardo. Ricardo was a financial specialist for a large division in a healthcare organization and had been identified as a succession candidate—someone who might one day take the reins. However, his boss called me and said, "Ricardo's ambition is causing some breakdowns in his relationships. We think he's a successor candidate, but if he can't get his ambition under control, he's going to stall in his career path."

Ricardo and I worked together for about nine months. I believe he would characterize the first ninety days as "torturous"—a bit more extreme than the "Why do you make my head hurt?" reaction I usually get from coaching clients. The reason the experience was so torturous for Ricardo was that it forced him to slow down and review his own behaviors and identify *all* the points where he wasn't operating from his authentic self. This didn't apply to just one relationship or project but to most of the people, initiatives, and strategies he worked on.

Broadly speaking, he had a high level of technical acumen, which was greatly respected; however, he proved difficult to work with, thanks to his know-it-all attitude. Technically speaking, he actually *did* know it all, but this left little to no room for *partnering* with others.

I had Ricardo mentally replay some business scenarios from his past and asked him, "How did you show up? What did you say? What assumptions were you making? What preferences did you have for how it should have happened?" He was a numbers guy, so I'd break it down quantitatively with a query like, "How many questions did you ask the other person during that interaction?" We did a great deal of deconstruction, with the aim of helping him realize what really occurred in those interactions. Just as important, we explored how the experience he generated had created the opposite impact he'd expected and needed to achieve his end goal.

There was one question that really tripped him up—"What did you notice in that moment about other people's reactions to what you were saying?" His answer: "Nothing. They didn't react." Of course, the other person *was* having a reaction; Ricardo simply wasn't being attentive to it. He had a fair reason: he was already figuring out the next steps to the solution of the problem in his head, so he'd be talking it through the whole time, leaving no pause for the other person to react. This illuminated a moment of friction. Next, I asked him, "How do *you* feel when somebody talks at you and leaves no space for you to react?"

That was the first crack in the armor. Up until that point, Ricardo hadn't done any of the compassionate honesty with himself that would allow him to recognize that *he* could play a part in the negative experience he was having and contributing to the disconnect from the other person. The sticking point in this case is that Ricardo was right. He was the know-it-all who really *did* know it all. The technical expertise was there. He had the stats to prove it. The problem was that he had no humility about the fact that his potential partners *also* had valuable expertise—and was thus eliminating all chances of partnering.

Ricardo and I walked through six months of meetings and projects that had felt uncomfortable to him. Again and again, scenarios like the one just described arose. In the rearview mirror, he could see that, when he'd tried to accomplish something, it had often halted because the relationships he had with the other individuals involved weren't respectful. That was an adjustment he had to make.

Think back to your own career. Have you ever worked with a Ricardo? Alternatively, have you ever found yourself having disconnects with people who were supposed to be professional partners—and not sure why?

It's never fun to look in the mirror and think, *I did this to myself.* That's why Ricardo found that experience so torturous. And that's why it's so hard to operate from a place of greater authenticity—because authenticity means operating from a place of greater vulnerability. In the corporate world, that can be seen as a negative. But it doesn't have to be.

Dr. Timothy R. Clark has a wonderful way of framing this phenomenon. He calls it "rewarded vulnerability." Vulnerability creates a space for others to be vulnerable, which promotes psychological safety. This is what people need to truly communicate, connect, and collaborate. Ricardo began to accept that a little humble pie—some vulnerability—was going to take him a very long way in his partnerships and his career.

This speaks to an ability to live in a state of Generative Wholeness™. Generative Wholeness™ is a state of being that empowers a person to sustain excellence, from the inside out. Wholeness *arises* from being generative. It's what allows a person to step into life in new ways consciously and to change. By living in the state of being that is Generative Wholeness™, it's possible to consistently choose changes that are positive and that nurture vitality.

Generative Wholeness™ means adopting the dynamic capacities to originate, create, learn, and produce results so that we live in a sovereign state, with the freedom to express personally and professionally from our inner authentic self.

> **Generative Wholeness™ means adopting the dynamic capacities to originate, create, learn, and produce results so that we live in a sovereign state, with the freedom to express personally and professionally from our inner authentic self.**

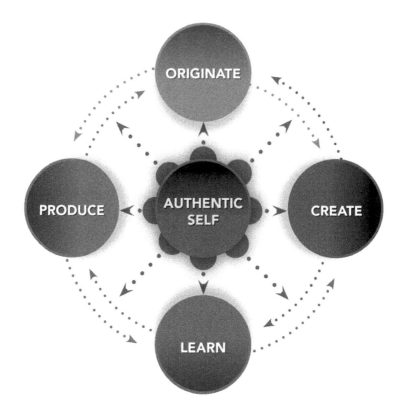

Generative Wholeness™ is the purpose of this whole book. Rather than saving that objective for the final chapter, I want to start by presenting you with the end goal, the beautiful meadow that is possible once you've learned the skills discussed in this book—skills like realizing your context, recognizing what you don't know, exercising proactive reflection, tolerating the presence of tension, appreciating common leadership dilemmas, and exercising deliberate judgment. The end result is, hopefully, that you are able to live as your authentic self and exist in a state of Generative Wholeness™.

Trusting the Unknown: The Gateway to Generative Wholeness™

I feel the deepest gratitude when a coaching client opens themselves up to the vulnerability of not knowing. Seeing beyond our comfortable preferences and biases is the only way we learn and grow. That requires *noticing*—and often, we must *learn* to notice. What do I mean by *learning to notice*? I'll give you an example of how I've experienced it, both through a client and within myself.

I was working with a CEO, Johnathan, who hired me because he wanted to leave the organization he was with. He was planning to exit within six months. At least, that's what he said. But about thirty days into our work, I said to him, "You're not ready to leave, are you?" He laughed and said, "You have totally turned my head around." I asked, "Is that a good thing or a bad thing?" He replied honestly: "I'm not sure yet."

Through our work together, we discovered that Johnathan was disempowering his executive team. He'd send them five-page white papers forty-eight hours before a meeting and then show up to the meeting and wonder why there was no discussion in the room—not considering that each member of his team had their own workload and pace and that forty-eight hours may not have been enough time to give these white papers the thought they were due. He wasn't pulling back to consider that bigger picture; he was just tired of *his* experience of having no discussion in the room. He felt his team wasn't engaged, so he thought he was done.

From an operational standpoint, Johnathan was a very successful leader, well regarded as an industry expert and a champion for change. He had a great vision on how to navigate that change, and he wanted his team to share that vision. But while *he* was trusting the unknown, open to trying innovative approaches to deal with industry shifts, his team wasn't—and he wasn't giving them any room to do so. He had no idea what they knew or didn't know. He was responding to the tension he felt with technical acumen, which wasn't wrong but also wasn't addressing the whole story. He wasn't *noticing*.

Identifying that gap was the first step. Then, we started making progress, and he was a lot happier. He didn't leave the organization after six months, as he'd first planned. He stayed on, and we continued to work together.

We were about three years into our coaching relationship when we hit a new thorny problem—again, *noticing* was the key to solving it. In this case, I was the one who failed to take notice of the thorn as quickly as I should have.

Before each of our coaching sessions, Johnathan and I would have lunch and catch up. Then, we'd walk down this long hallway to his office to start the session. One day, we were walking down that hallway to his office, and my stomach was upset. Normally I wouldn't have given this much thought, but it was the third time this had happened. My body was telling me something. I spoke up, revealing to Johnathan that when we walked down the hallway to his office, I was feeling sick to my stomach, and that it wasn't the first time. He had this sparkle in his eye as he chuckled and said, "Same here."

I was surprised. My reaction was along the lines of, "What the heck?! Why didn't you say anything?" That's when he revealed that he was ready to push our coaching work to the next level of depth, something he'd been afraid to tell me up until then. He said, "I've been nervous to tell you, because I like the work we're doing now, but I feel like there's more we can do. There's something wanting."

That was a lesson to me. I hadn't been paying enough attention; I failed to notice that he was ready to go deeper. I thought it was all about me when, in fact, it was about both of us and about our coaching relationship. It wasn't until it smacked me upside the head, until the third time when I walked down the hallway and had that sick-to-my-stomach feeling, that I finally took notice and gave a voice to my discomfort.

In that instance, taking notice allowed us to push further. It opened the door to trusting the unknown and exploring new depths in our coaching. The payoff was huge. I'm very glad we took notice and grateful that my client opened himself up to the possibility of not knowing. Johnathan ended up not only staying on with his organization, but he also helped commandeer one of the most successful acquisitions in the history of his industry.

> Can you think of a time when you failed to notice—perhaps your own discontent or that of someone in your team? Alternatively, maybe you can think of a time when you felt someone else wasn't picking up on the signals you were sending.

HOW LEARNING TO NOTICE BUILDS RESILIENCE

That act of noticing is critical to tolerating the presence of tension, which we'll look at more closely in chapter 4. You've got to notice sandpaper moments, instances of friction, before they become destructive. Otherwise, if you rub sandpaper on something long enough, you'll wear the object away completely.

Johnathan was on the brink when I first met him. He'd already drafted his resignation letter. However, we were able to notice the presence of tension—first, in his relationship with his team and then in our coaching relationship. We then sat in that tension instead of speeding past it, which allowed us to push toward a positive resolution and a profitable innovation.

> **The act of noticing is critical to tolerating the presence of tension.**

I often compare this process to stretching and relaxing a rubber band. You want to keep your rubber band resilient, which means you can stretch it out and relax it, stretch it out and relax it—on and on. You're controlling the tension in the rubber band. But you have to think, "What's just the right amount of tension to keep moving forward? How much tension is too much; when do I need to slow down, let the rubber band relax, and get my resilience back?"

That state of being is always changing, and it's up to you to *notice* those changes. The noticing is what sets you up to let go and trust the unknown—because you know that you're paying attention and can manipulate the rubber band before it stretches or relaxes too much.

Now, trusting the unknown often means letting go of what's comfortable. Growth requires freeing yourself from the familiar. Think of a potted plant. As it grows, its root network becomes more intricate and deeper. It needs a new pot to thrive. It has to leave behind the familiarity of its little pot and trust in the unknown—that the bigger pot will have the soil, the nutrients, and the sunshine that it needs to thrive.

This is where we humans tend to get into trouble. We don't trust in the unknown, like that little potted plant. We overthink. We analyze. We retreat. We come back to what we know and find what's comfortable. We revert to our old lens. How do we adapt that lens?

Sovereignty can help. When you come from a place of sovereignty and you're facing the unknown, you will be able to recognize the experience, education, and technical acumen you possess. You will be able to see that you have the tools you need to thrive. Remember, even plants store nutrients in their roots. When you're moving that potted plant to a new pot, it's not starting from zero. Neither are you.

However, to really trust in the unknown, you've got to take it a step further. You must recognize the limits of those tools in the current context. How do you know which aspects of your experience, education, and technical acumen will be useful and relevant to the situation in *front* of you, to the future that feels like it will be very different? You want to be fit for *that* future—and that future is unknown.

If you do the same thing over and over again, regardless of the context that you find yourself in, it's going to stop working. As time evolves, your approach will no longer match the situation. Again, that's when noticing becomes so essential—you've got to see those changes and then trust in the unknown to navigate them, because you won't be able to take the exact same approach as before—not successfully.

I've seen this problem arise frequently with sales professionals who get promoted from a boots-on-the-ground role to a management position. They get the promotion because they're making great numbers, not necessarily because they know how to lead effectively. One woman in particular comes to mind, a senior vice president (VP) of US sales for a medical device company. I'll call her Cassandra.

Cassandra was on a high potential path, being gradually groomed for a C-suite role—say, five to seven years down the road. The company was really investing in her and even considering putting her through an executive MBA program. As part of her development, they asked me to coach her.

Now, Cassandra had made it so far in her career in part because, of course, she had great sales figures. She was a fantastic closer. She could close practically any deal, no matter how prickly it seemed. She was confident in her abilities and rightfully so. However, she was less confident in entrusting "the close" to others.

This was largely because she had distinct biases about what made for a high-performance salesperson—biases we had to unveil in conversation. I'd ask her what she considered the characteristics of a high-performance salesperson. Not surprisingly, Cassandra's idea of what made for a high-performance salesperson were traits she herself had. She was rewarding people in her team with those traits, without making space for others who had different strengths.

Due to her lack of trust in anyone who didn't fit her ideal sales-person mold, Cassandra tended to overstep. When it came time to close a deal, she'd swoop in and close it—because she was confident that she could (and she was right). This created issues in her team. She was disempowering the other individuals, for one thing, and—if you want to get down to dollars and cents—she was preventing them from collecting on a valuable commission. Understandably, people were frustrated.

Cassandra's transformation was one that many leaders must go through. She had to learn how to go from *doing* to *managing*. She had to be able to step back and let go. She had to trust and empower her team to close. This couldn't be achieved through blind trust. Rather, the shift started with Cassandra learning about her team members as whole people instead of engaging with them only when the pursuit of a deal required it.

At first, Cassandra was scared to let go of her role as the "ace in the hole" for closing deals, because that was how she made sure goals were met and everyone received bonuses, one of the key extrinsic motivators for salespeople. Transforming into a management mindset required her to think more about intrinsic motivation and her responsibility to build a team.

These were all things we worked on in our coaching relationship. It was a difficult path, requiring her to change her base mindset and, in tandem, her actions. And that change required her to trust in the unknown. She had to have faith that the changes she made would net the results she wanted—a better relationship with her sales team and greater team member autonomy, along with desirable sales figures.

> **Pause. Have you ever worked with a Cassandra? Alternatively, is there any aspect of her character that you can identify with?**

Trusting the unknown is always going to push the edges of how you think. This requires energy, which means it's important that, when you step onto the path of growth, you make space for it. Trusting in the unknown can help reframe your mindset and embrace the fact that Generative Wholeness™ is a continual state of being—not a single transformation that you complete once and move on from. Adopting the dynamic capacities that are being generative—creating, learning, producing, and originating—will equip you to confidently anticipate, recognize, and respond to change as it emerges.

Generative Wholeness™ Restores Access to Personal Essence

Generative Wholeness™ is a state of being that empowers a person to sustain excellence from the inside out. The word "generative" is a puzzle to many people, but if you take a look in the dictionary, it's pretty straightforward: it simply means continuously producing results. Creation comes from new, original thinking. You let yourself use your imagination and your intuition to bring something forward that is a variation on a theme or something nobody's ever thought of before. That original idea gets created and tested, so you can learn what's most useful and satisfying and then produce that product, solution, or experience. That flow I've just described is being generative.

Being generative empowers four capacities: to originate new thinking; create something tangible from that imagination; experiment to learn what is most valuable; and ultimately, to produce outcomes for yourself and others that contribute to success, well-being, and a thriving life.

I see being generative as a double helix. One strand builds those four capacities I've just mentioned. In turn, a second strand radiates from the inside out, honoring the unique soul of each person—the traits that express their essence, their authentic self. This better equips the individual to face their inner critic—the rule maker and judge that counters their essence. Every day, you have a tension between expressing your essence and your inner critic.

Think of your inner critic now. When is the last time that voice was activated? What did it tell you? How did you react to it?

A significant mindset shift comes when you start to treat your inner critic as an ally. So, instead of your inner critic judging, diminishing, or shutting you down, it might ask, "Are you really sure you want to do that?" That's not a put-down. It's just a respectful question that causes you to reflect whether the action you are considering will honor who you are as a human.

That's the kind of mindset shift that happens in coaching. Through conversation and reflection, you open up the aperture of your camera lens and start to recognize that the things that seem to hold you back can actually be useful. The result is a shift in four parts: identity, experience, action, and outcome. An example can help demonstrate what I mean.

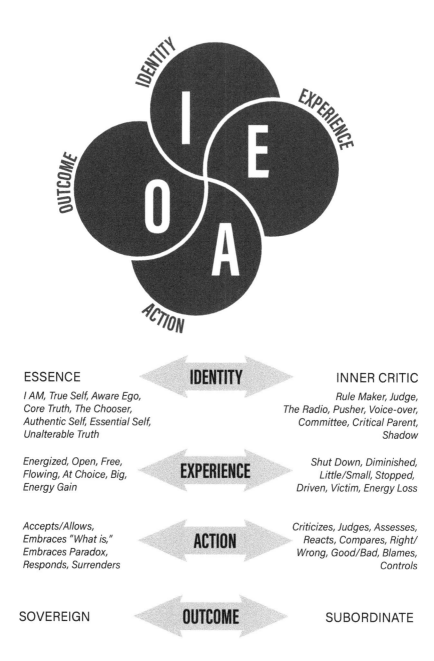

I worked with a woman who was responsible for marketing and advertising in a global pharmaceutical company. I'll call her Maria. She had twins, about four years old, and she was struggling with the stress of leaving them constantly for work travel. However, that's not where our coaching relationship began. It began with a conversation about her team meetings. In her view, her team wasn't bringing sufficient creativity to their meetings. I had to help her figure out why that was.

Maria and I spent a lot of time talking about work—in fact, she seemed to want to speak only about work, even after we'd had many meetings together, by which point some personal details about a person's life usually tend to emerge. At one point, I asked her, "What do you notice is missing in our conversations? If you think about your wholeness, if you think about your whole life, what are the points we rarely touch on?" She sat quietly for a long time and finally said, "I rarely tell you anything about my family."

We pulled on that thread. Maria revealed that, as a senior executive, she felt she could no longer be as personal with her team.

She was holding back a part of her identity that she was very passionate about—her family. She traveled frequently for work, and, as she recounted saying goodbye to her twins for a trip, she got a little teary-eyed.

We pulled on that thread a little more. Eventually, Maria realized that her concern for her children missing her—feeling a maternal lack while she was traveling for work—was transferring to a motherly concern for her team. Her intentions were good. She didn't want her team to struggle or suffer, so she was always anticipating the next move, but she acknowledged that she was probably mothering them as a result. She began to see that the reason her team wasn't showing up as creatively as she wanted was because she was smothering them.

So, how could Maria navigate that sticky situation? In her case, the answer came from acknowledging the rift between her professional and personal lives, a rift that was causing her deep pain. She acknowledged, "I want to be able to have a personal relationship with my team. I want them to know all of who I am. I want them to feel comfortable with my expressive joy and know that theirs can also be expressed in the same way."

That is wholeness. It took connecting to her whole self for Maria to recognize that the shame she was feeling about being away from her twins was getting "solved" by caretaking her team, which was causing them to underperform. Once she tapped into her wholeness, her relationship to herself and to those around her shifted. She let herself share her identity as a mother at work. She stopped caretaking her team, instead moving into the role of coach and mentor and making space for others to take agency and express creativity.

Maria's case exemplifies the benefits of noticing the inner voices that influence you. As you claim and embody the traits of your authentic self, others experience this when engaged with you. For some, this feels like permission to do the same. Generally, expressing greater authenticity, especially as a role model, positively affects morale, engagement, productivity, and loyalty. However, for others, the change may feel unsettling.

As a leader, noticing the impact will prepare you to engage transparently. This change within you will be noticed by others. Sharing your experience creates a workplace climate that encourages each person to notice within themselves the parts of their wholeness they want to more fully express. Keep the end goal in mind—to realize and maximize potential in every person. This requires every person to remember, claim, and embody the traits and qualities that represent their essence.

As a generative leader, you embrace your own wholeness and encourage others to live in wholeness as well. Conversely, when leaders are not generative, when they deny their own wholeness, they also subvert the wholeness of others.

Think of Maria's story. Have you ever worked with someone like Maria? Did you ever wonder what might impact their approach to their team?

WHY I'M WARY OF "TRANSFORMATION"

I'm not manufacturing some new model here. The elements we've explored so far—sovereignty, authentic self, essence, being generative, and wholeness—are what I've observed from my work with thousands of leaders and their teams over nearly three decades. I've noticed patterns of behavior in those individuals and organizations. I've seen how those behaviors have impacted performance in their respective organizations and whether they have (or haven't) produced results.

Through these observations, I've found that the state of being generative seems to be firmly rooted in the four capacities I described.

I've further found that Generative Wholeness™ as a state of being seems to be an effective way of handling thorny problems not only at work but also in the world at large.

At the same time, I've discovered that "transformation"—a common term in organizational change discussions—is too simple an approach. Transformation implies a change of state. Instead of focusing on the *state*, I want to focus on the *way of being*. This paves the path to a more fluid and adaptive approach. It's more sustainable, too.

Instead of committing to the grandiose idea of transformation, consider how you might sustain a way of being that has you comfortable being adaptive. Transformation is too situation-specific. Generative Wholeness™, in contrast, is all about building capacity and, with it, resilience. It's about giving you greater control over that rubber band I mentioned and how much tension it holds.

This is why sovereignty is so important. It's an internal choice to notice that the environment is changing. It's happening right now. Where you get into trouble is that you fail to notice things shifting right underneath your feet. Then, what could have been a small change is suddenly a big change. Everything becomes a crisis. Generative Wholeness™ reduces the drama: your sensory system is acute enough to recognize the shifts. You're prepared to *notice*.

It's like sailing. You're tacking as the winds shift. You're constantly navigating your course. It may not be the direct line as a crow would fly, because you have to be responsive to the shift in the winds—as well as the shifts in the currents and tides. It requires multifaceted and continual adaptation. If you aren't noticing those changes, you risk getting off course. If you aren't trusting in the unknown and acknowledging your abilities to navigate those changes, you risk getting stuck. And if you haven't built up your generative capacity, that constant flux may leave you exhausted.

But if you're operating from a state of Generative Wholeness™, you'll notice the changes. You'll trust in the unknown and in your abilities to navigate the unknown. Consider the anecdotes of Ricardo, Cassandra, and Maria. At first, none of these leaders was operating from a state of wholeness. Ricardo was steamrolling his partners. Cassandra was unable to empower her team. Maria had a massive rift in her personal and professional lives, which led to her mothering her team. If you, like these leaders, can learn to trust in the unknown and adapt to your changing environment, you'll find it much easier to stay on course.

The Reflective Power of Generative Wholeness™

One of the biggest issues I see in organizations arises from failing to learn—and that often starts with leaders. Companies spend millions of dollars on *learning*. There's even a role for it: chief learning officer. However, often these roles are overly academic, exclusively strategy focused, and/or too underfunded to actually drive shifts that will impact the workforce and, by extension, the customer experience.

All too often, leaders embrace learning initiatives as an expense rather than an investment. They look at stats, facts, and figures instead of letting *wonder* lead the way. They don't trust in the unknown or ask what's possible if they try a different way. A learning mindset—about the people companies so carefully recruit, select, and hire—becomes the key to unlocking the hidden potential in the workforce.

> Have you ever witnessed an organizational learning initiative utterly fail? What reasons were given for the flop at the time? Reexamining the situation now, were those reasons valid?

When leaders choose to learn about the essence of each team member, they can identify the sources of interference to maximizing their potential. That interference most directly occurs when values conflict, when calcified thinking and beliefs operate as acceptable bias, and when destructive leadership behaviors are tolerated.

Leaders must notice and unpack the "known" in order to examine how it imbues organizational beliefs. That means being prepared to *un-learn* in order to notice something new and useful—and allow it to emerge. Learning is often deconstructing. Leaders need to reflect—for example, to realize their inherent bias and recognize what they don't know. Only then can they reconstruct to produce something different.

There are positive examples of learning in organizations, such as listening circles, where leaders talk to parts of the organization they don't normally talk to and create a safe space for personnel to speak up. For example, the leader may ask, "What's happening for you and your work, team, project?"—whatever the case may be. This creates space for reflection.

In the corporate world, there's a mindset that time spent on reflection is not productive. It's not moving something to market. However, failing to reflect leaves a lot of money on the table. It may be invisible on the profit-and-loss (P&L) statement, but it's visible to others in the form of destructive leader behaviors that contribute to incivility, poor employee engagement, and subpar productivity. The sad fact is that the consequence of not taking the time to do this reflective work—to *learn*—means repeating histories of underperformance and untapped potential.

Now, that doesn't mean homing in on the negatives of history (another common misstep). There is often a lot of good to learn when reflecting on an initiative's outcomes. Instead of calling such meetings "post-mortems," which suggests someone died, why not call them learning insights or insights meetings? Focus on the positives. Ask, "What did we activate in the organization that was a capacity we didn't use before? How do we repeat that because that was super successful? Where did we fall into old patterns, not realizing that they weren't the right fit? What caused us to do that? What did we not pay attention to?" Such questioning is all about practicing the micro-skill of reflection.

REFLECTING ON THE EVOLVING NATURE OF WORK

Taking a minute to reflect is usually more efficient and cost-effective than barreling ahead without reflection. Corporate messes are very expensive to rework, especially in a world where change occurs rapidly. And I mean "expensive" not only in a dollars-and-cents way. Say you wait until there's a breakdown to reflect. That takes a huge emotional, mental, physical, and spiritual toll on the teams who have done something that didn't work because their boss didn't pay attention to the changing environment.

That can impact the conditions of satisfaction in the work environment—which aren't great. As of 2023, 98 percent of people on the job are looking for another

> **Taking a minute to reflect is usually more efficient and cost-efficient than barreling ahead.**

job.[8] Gallup's 2023 "State of the Global Workplace" report reveals that a mere 23 percent of employees are "thriving" at work and actively engaged. Meanwhile, 18 percent are loud quitting, and a whopping 59 percent are quiet quitting.[9]

These statistics and their context change over time. However, they point to broader trends of dissatisfaction between employers and employees—something you'll always find, regardless of the decade. In 2023, one of the biggest issues being touted is the rise of the hybrid workforce. Who knows what the issue will be in 2033, 2043, and beyond. It may be something we can't even identify yet. There will always be *something* that people are responding to that's impacting workforces.

Knowing this, the companies that are going to succeed are the ones that already have a strong relationship with their folks. This allows them to recognize when a new force is going to impact workers in some way and to determine how to get ahead of it. Managers who are prepared to sustain social connection and help people remember their wholeness are the ones who will thrive, regardless of the circumstances.

One common issue I've seen is that leaders hire people because they see a competency match with a job role—and then promptly assimilate their new hires into the organization and discount the unique attributes those individuals were hired for. That doesn't leave workers feeling seen or valued. The fallout was first seen with the millennial generation changing jobs every 2.8 years on average.[10] That's

---

8   Jessica Dickler, "96% of Workers Are Looking for a New Job in 2023, Poll Says," CNBC, January 13, 2023, https://www.cnbc.com/2023/01/13/96percent-of-workers-are-looking-for-a-new-job-in-2023.html.

9   "State of the Global Workplace: 2023 Report," Gallup, 2023, https://www.gallup.com/workplace/349484/state-of-the-global-workplace.aspx.

10   "How Long Do Millennials Stay on the Job?" Zippia, June 29, 2022, https://www.zippia.com/answers/how-long-do-millennials-stay-at-a-job/.

not healthy for employers, and it's expensive. Meanwhile, employees aren't getting a chance to get their feet under them. They're searching for employers who will invest in them and give them opportunities to demonstrate that they're worthy of that investment. When those things are lacking, they leave.

> **Pause. Can you remember a time when you were eager to escape a job? What was the reason? Was it money? A lack of responsibility? A toxic work environment? A difficult boss? What conditions of satisfaction weren't being met?**

Employers may complain about what they call "entitlement," but they also have to recognize that they are largely responsible for the conditions of satisfaction in the experience the employee has. Get that formula right, and the result is satisfied, self-responsible employees—and, in most cases, happy employees translate to happy customers.[11]

Many companies fail to get that formula right because bosses want results, and they look at results as numbers. They aren't looking at the human beings who are getting the work done. They aren't taking enough time to reflect on the people and processes or opening themselves up to trusting in the unknown and reflecting on what's gone wrong with their workforce. They just want a neat and tidy report with great quarterly earnings and a solid P&L statement.

---

11   Andrew Chamberlain and Daniel Zhao, "The Key to Happy Customers? Happy Employees," *Harvard Business Review*, August 19, 2019, https://hbr.org/2019/08/the-key-to-happy-customers-happy-employees.

These leaders aren't living in a state of Generative Wholeness™ that maximizes their potential. At the same time, they aren't allowing those around them to embody their unique essence—and realize *their* maximum potential. Remember, by being generative, we collectively produce the conditions by which each person enthusiastically accepts responsibility to live in their wholeness, accessing and using all of their potential.

I believe that Generative Wholeness™ can serve anybody. However, I think it's particularly important for the leaders who have such a significant impact on working environments. As the world of work changes ever more rapidly, thanks to new technologies like artificial intelligence (AI), it will become all the more important for leaders to pause and reflect on the decisions they make about how to show up, interact, and make decisions with their team and colleagues.

There Is No Generative Wholeness™ without Patience

The way we work is changing quickly. The environment is evolving: the premise of the work we're doing has changed; the circumstances around that work have changed; the players have changed. We must adapt and remain adaptive. Generative Wholeness™ is one way.

You won't reach a state of Generative Wholeness™ overnight. Patience is needed to get there—and, ironically, patience is a big part of Generative Wholeness™. Patience requires the acceptance that *you* might be some part, cause, or agent of what's going on with you and those around you. Like Ricardo, Cassandra, Maria, or Johnathan, you'll be stuck until you can acknowledge this.

Patience is often undervalued in the business world, where efficiency is prioritized. But patience is becoming increasingly important as we learn to navigate the thorny problems of the modern work environment. Still, in a lot of fast-moving corporate environments, we have it drilled into us that, if a result isn't met, we must figure out why quickly. It's a blame-and-shame game. Pinpoint a person or a team, and let them be the scapegoat. The problem is, it's always possible to find (or create) a scapegoat, which means systemic issue(s) are never examined.

The alternative is to have a little bit of patience with things that didn't turn out the way you wanted them to. You always want to be able to sustain excellence. However, because the world is always changing—the earth shifting beneath our feet—it's hard to do if you don't pause for a minute and say, "Hey, what's changed? How might that cause me to recalibrate the rubric I'm using to choose what actions I take?"

Leaders will grapple with understanding the habits, preferences, assumptions, and biases that are driving the decisions they make, until they can sit in the discomfort of stillness. I'm not talking about pausing for weeks at a time. I'm talking about a pause of twenty-four hours, long enough to consider that maybe you don't have the whole story.

Can you sit in the tension of inaction? It feels uncomfortable because your habit is to stay in motion. If you can suspend that habit for just a little longer, can you sit in the discomfort? Patience is what gives you the opportunity to sit in the presence of tension and then rethink how to navigate that tension.

Patience is also what allows you to pull back for perspective. Pulling back is important if you're going to look beyond that limited lens of yours and take in the bigger picture. Instead of just glancing in the rearview mirror of the car, you'll be able to look out the front windshield toward the horizon and see the myriad of possibilities it holds. For that to happen, you've got to pull back—and that isn't always easy. Let's talk about it in chapter 3.

EXERCISE: TAKE A MOMENT TO REFLECT

You've noticed a situation, initiative, or key stakeholder relationship that continually stimulates your impatience. Use this noticing as your opportunity to hit pause and practice shifting your mindset toward greater patience. Hang on to your responses—you'll come back to them in the end-of-chapter exercises for chapters 5 and 6.

1. Alignment: Think to the beginning of the process. Consider what the basis was for choosing those actions that didn't produce the result you expected. The basis is often a value or principle—you might look back to the exercise in chapter 1 for inspiration.

2. Clarity: Notice the internal motivation or stimulus for wanting to make those choices. This is often a belief.

3. Awareness: Now, notice what data, information, experience, or perspectives were dismissed or discounted—and now seem relevant for a new, more empowering choice.

CHAPTER 3

PULL BACK FOR PERSPECTIVE

The obvious is not obvious. It is constructed.
—DAVE GRAY, AUTHOR OF *LIMINAL THINKING:*
CREATE THE CHANGE YOU WANT BY CHANGING THE WAY
YOU THINK

Pulling back for perspective simply means pulling back and looking at all the elements that influence you and your habits, biases, and reactions. However, that "big picture" starts much smaller—with simply pulling back and looking at *yourself*. This requires understanding who you are and how that perspective of yourself motivates your decisions and actions. You can then identify patterns that generate peaks and plateaus in your life, both personal and professional.

Archetypes can be a wonderful starting point for leaders—or anyone, really—to start untangling their view of themselves, the world, and their place in it. There's a lot happening inside of you. Wouldn't you like to know what is silently and invisibly operating below your surface? Archetypes can help you do just that. And archetypes go beyond yourself. An understanding of archetypes is a wonderful way to better understand those around you. Archetypes can thus also help you understand your interactions with others, minimizing the risks of misunderstandings and miscommunications.

According to the co-founders of the Archetypes at Work™ method, Richard Olivier and Dr. Laurence Hill, an understanding of the most common archetypes helps people to engage with personal, professional, and cultural development—especially in an increasingly complex world. Bringing the ancient into modern time brings the best of human patterns into current relevance, serving as a resource to reset and restore harmony while leaders learn to navigate uncertainty and accelerating complexity.

Focusing on thorny problems through an archetypal eye has a number of advantages. It's developed through an embodied approach and learned through lived experience. Pulling back allows each person to see their life on a stage, with internal actors that learn to spontane- ously adapt to a dynamic environment with greater ease. An example can help illuminate the value.

Archetypes as a Starting Point

I was once talking to an executive—I'll call him John—who had a person on his team who was a very introverted processor. I'll call her Tara. Tara was a thoughtful woman, brilliant but quiet. In a large group, she didn't speak much. She often wouldn't speak at all unless invited to speak. When she *did* speak, it would just be a few words, but those words would usually be quite profound. They added value.

However, John was getting frustrated with Tara. He took her reticence to talk as lack of involvement. In light of an upcoming restructuring, he was ready to fire her. I told him, "I think you have a gem in Tara. As your reorganization unfolds in the next three months, be very thoughtful about drawing her out and finding out what her point of view is. Don't be impatient with her inability to do it in the large group. Find ways for her to do it with you one-on-one or in smaller group settings."

That's exactly what John did. He sat down with Tara in a one-on-one, and he had one of the most productive meetings he'd had in ages. At the end of the meeting, he asked her, "Can we see more of this when you're in a large group?" She offered to try.

John had been on the brink of firing Tara when, in fact, she was absolutely the right person for the job. They simply embodied drastically different archetypal energies in their daily activities. Tara was a strategic thinker, the kind that often gets overlooked in our legacy demand for charisma. John was a charismatic speaker, the kind that is sometimes characterized as a bully.

John could have steamrolled Tara; instead, he slowed down and recognized the difference in how they processed things. In doing so, he fulfilled the old adage that the whole is greater than the sum of parts. The point here is that without patience to pull back, everyone would have suffered—the leader (John), the worker (Tara), and the enterprise as a whole. The organization could have suffered the loss of Tara and John's combined brain power and emotional energy. Instead, these two exemplary individuals were able to work in synergy.

 Put yourself in John's shoes. Who's the Tara on your team? How do you communicate with them? What might you do differently? Alternatively, have you ever felt like the Tara in this story—or maybe you still do?

There are ten essential archetypes, and understanding yours can help you understand how you relate to the people around you and, hopefully, interact with them in more productive ways. Others have done fantastic work in this field, including Carolyn Myss, Carol Pearson, and Dr. James Hillman. If you're looking for a good introduction to the archetypes, I'd recommend Lawrence Hillman and Richard Olivier's *Archetypes at Work: Evolving Your Story, One Character at a Time.*

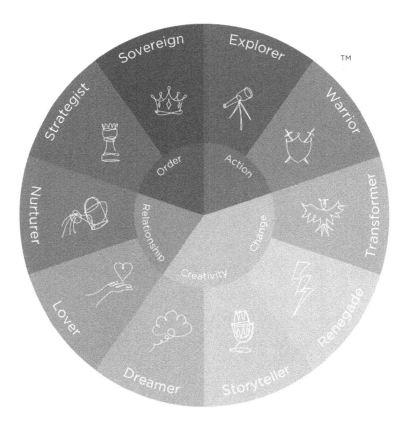

John was expressing from the Strategist and Warrior archetypes, while Tara was likely preferring to embody the energies of the Explorer and Transformer. Identifying those differences is what allowed John to find value in Tara despite not at first understanding her. It's what allowed him to figure out what made her tick. However, he had to start with figuring out what made *him* tick.

All ten archetypes live within every person, and we build habits and preferences unconsciously that keep us from tapping into all the energies. What we don't embody in ourselves causes blank spaces in our ability to perceive others' energy. It's like they're the actors in the wings of the theater stage; we don't see them, so we are at risk of discounting them. Constructing an internal archetypal eye expands our view of self and then our view of everyone else, allowing us to notice potential and learn to activate energies we might otherwise leave off stage, in the wings.

Archetypal "Eye" versus Archetypal Voice: Informing the Four Tensions Operating Inside of You

In my view, the Archetypes at Work™ method extends beyond the "archetypal eye," to borrow Hillman and Olivier's language, to include an archetypal voice. What's the language choice that a leader uses when they are preparing the story of a strategy? What's the language choice they use when they want to be nurturing to their team without seeming disingenuous? How do they communicate their message? What does a leader allow themselves to perceive that's beyond their own voice? Do they receive the messages delivered from their team leaders that are expressed in a way other than their preferred archetypal energies?

This learning expands a leader's ability to perceive that voice both in themselves and in others. Once those voices are identified, it's about being able to work with the common human patterning and finding a voice that matches both the audience and the circumstance. Versatility, fluidity, and spontaneity abound when a leader chooses to embody all ten archetypes all the time.

This again raises the diversity and inclusion piece I touched on in the first chapter. Recognizing and speaking to archetypes help draw others out and create psychological safety in their interactions. It allows other people to recognize that they're deeply seen, felt, and understood. With that safety, challenge doesn't feel personal. If a leader questions an individual, that individual won't retreat. Rather, the challenge of a question can focus on *ideas*, allowing something creative to emerge.

An understanding of the archetypal eye and the archetypal voice as energies expressed can also help people navigate basic life tensions, like that of sovereignty versus performance. I've talked a bit about sovereignty and self-ruling—the idea of accepting responsibility for the inner authority to choose how we want to relate to our lives. In contrast, performance is about deploying our inner authority and capacity to meet some external expectation.

> **Recognizing and speaking to someone's archetype makes them feel deeply seen, felt, and understood.**

Now, this isn't a bad thing; humans *have* to do that. It's part of existing in the world. When I speak to a room full of people, that's a performance act. How I prepare for that speech is a sovereign act. When I'm speaking in front of the room, I need to be able to perform. I need to speak in a cadence that works and have some variability in my delivery. However, I also need to realize that the people in attendance are there to experience *me*, as an individual, which means

I probably need a bit more sovereignty than performance. A rehearsed talk, no matter how well rehearsed, is still a written talk. It doesn't account for energy, which is what resonates with the audience and creates a relationship with them.

Sovereignty and performance are one of the tensions constantly operating inside of us humans. The four tensions mentioned next are common to all humankind. They're operating all the time, as general life tensions, felt but largely invisible—until you start to scratch the surface.

The executive I mentioned earlier, John, had his own struggles with sovereignty and performance. He was overseeing a time of transition in his organization, which was proving to be tumultuous. In the thick of it, a colleague of his—I'll call him Darrell—referred to John as a "bully," a big, nasty word with a lot of negative implications.

As John and I talked through the situation, concrete issues started to crystallize. Darrell was undermining John outside of meetings, gossiping and misrepresenting conversations and agreements. John had to tighten the reins on timelines, resources, and focus to successfully guide the organization through the tumultuous transition. Unfortunately, John was also reacting to the name-calling by shutting down. He would show up to meetings, and, instead of using curiosity with his questions, he'd use closed, evaluative questions (e.g., "Is this done yet?" and "Have you got the project back on track?"). That direct approach doesn't allow for learning and tends to further shut down people. Team members don't feel psychological safety by their ideas and perspective being omitted from the conversation. Naturally, that deters them from bringing anything creative, innovative, or productive forward.

The relationship between John and Darrell deteriorated, as John continued to act from a place of pure performance instead of sovereignty. At the same time, overall morale took a hit. The workers viewing John were not recognizing the full story, so they were judging him inappropriately and buying into the "bully" narrative Darrell expressed at every chance. While that's not fair, such scenarios aren't uncommon—and they tend to create mistrust in the whole system.

Luckily, through our coaching interactions, John began to notice the impact of his choices and started to catch himself in the moment so that he could use a more open and curious approach. He was able to see the pattern of behavior beyond the words that was his habit and preference—that's the archetypal eye. He then found his archetypal voice that could express from the Strategist and Warrior archetypes and call forward his essence and harness his inherent strengths. He was able to shift his understanding of himself and, with it, his understanding of his colleague, Darrell, who clearly wanted recognition for his valuable contribution. This was what then allowed John to shift his interactions with Darrell. While he was once perceived as a "bully," his use of more relationship-oriented energies shifted others' perceptions to see John as a generous and inclusive partner.

Put yourself back in John's shoes. Do you have a Darrell on your team? How might you shift your interactions with them? Alternatively, have you ever identified someone as a "bully" in the workplace? Did you ever consider what was informing their behavior—was there perhaps something hidden from your view at the root of it?

Looking beyond Archetypes to Perceive Patterns

I do think that archetypes can be very useful in deepening our self-understanding. The patterning of the human condition explained by archetypal psychology especially has relevance when situations arise that challenge anyone to see more fully and clearly than their preferences and habits reveal. Strengthening pattern recognition skills has become a body of work carried over from psychology into organizational development, with great rewards. The body of work on archetypes covers huge territory, with research done by people who have deeply studied the underlying psychology—so I'll leave them to untangle the intricacies. I simply wanted to raise the topic here, because I think it opens a broader discussion into patterns of human behavior—which is where I'd like to focus.

Now, I adore the body of work done around archetypes. Do I think it's useful? Yes. However, I've chosen not to get stuck in the model side of things. In fact, I'm trying to eliminate model language altogether, because I find that people use it as a shortcut.

People tend to cling to a typology. A friend who's always late might say, "Hey, I'm a Libra! It's because I'm an air sign!" This is an extreme example, but it speaks to a certain human truth of how we shape and cling to identity, even when that identity doesn't serve us well. A typology doesn't always give us the fluidity we need to adapt. It can limit learning. It can undermine our patience, making us too quick to react based on our perceived typology. In fact, the ancient system of archetypes transcends typology and liberates the unique expression within the overarching human patterns that archetypes represent. No person *is* an archetype. Instead, every person expresses archetypal energies, with the potential to embody those energies at will, spontaneously appropriate to any context.

I've found that 95 percent of coaching work comes back to identifying some pattern of human interaction and relating that has triggered a reaction. When we learn to witness and recognize human patterns of interaction and relating, our attention shifts toward understanding the underlying motivation behind the situation causing a reaction. There's some habit, preference, assumption, or bias at work that has impacted the individual's reaction in each circumstance. That reaction is never actually about the circumstance. The circumstance was just the catalyst.

When this happens to you, seize the opportunity. This is a chance for you to question yourself. Think: *Is my reaction justified? What's the truth of what's happening here? Do I have a memory that's been activated? Do I have something that I'm holding onto as a belief or a principle that is outdated and doesn't fit the context? What might I be missing as a result?*

Often, it's something historical, a difficult moment from your past. I've talked about these "sandpaper moments" before, moments of friction (usually unpleasant) that come up in life. They're often beyond your control.

> Pause. Take a deep breath. Think back— what was a sandpaper moment in your life? It could be personal or professional. You can probably name one off the top of your head in seconds—one of those gut-punch life moments, the ones you usually don't see coming. A life-altering car accident could be an extreme example, or your romantic partner leaving you by surprise—or getting fired when you least antici- pated it.

When you were in that moment, it likely felt raw, tender, tight, and tough to navigate. But now that you're on the other side of that moment, you may look at it in the rearview mirror and appreci- ate it—because it was a moment of growth. It's often the sandpaper experiences that expose a reaction and, maybe, cause us to question that reaction. In most cases I've seen, those reactions involve patterns of relating to other people.

Now, if you've worked on *learning to notice* and you're operating from a place of Generative Wholeness™, it gets easier to navigate those sandpaper moments. In some instances, you may even be attuned enough to see those moments coming.

This happened to me at one point in my career, when I was on the brink of getting fired. I was at home enjoying a quiet evening after work, and it just came to me: *they're going to fire me.* So, I acted. The next day, I went into my boss's office and broached the topic of me leaving—and, in the process, negotiated a solid severance package for myself. That was a sandpaper moment that I caught. I didn't have to get fired to experience it. I still got the friction of feeling that I didn't fit at that company. However, I could also trust myself enough to realize that was OK—I didn't have to fit at that company and could do something else instead.

Even if you don't catch your sandpaper moment, and it takes you by surprise, it still has value. It helps you wake up. You start to perceive patterns. The aperture of your lens as you view the world gets a little wider. You realize there's more happening around you than what you're immediately paying attention to. You wonder what might happen if you let just a little more in—even just 10 percent more. This starts to put you into that state of wonder I discussed in the introduction. You start thinking, *Can I be in the experience of something that's outside of what I've allowed myself to see?* And that's also a step toward reconstructing, which I have mentioned in my discussion of Generative Wholeness™ in the second chapter.

Through those moments, you learn to recognize that there are aspects of yourself that you're choosing to sit on the bench. Often, these moments are born of tragedy, illness, or loss. While that's undesirable, you can then experience a desirable outcome as you begin the journey of reclaiming aspects of your essence, bringing you nearer to Generative Wholeness™.

Appearance and Reappearance of Mental Blinders and Emotional Barriers

In the process of perceiving patterns, you usually also unveil what I call mental blinders and emotional barriers. These blinders and barriers keep the aperture of the lens through which you view the world (and yourself) small. In the process, they impede your growth.

If it's possible, pause a moment and look out the window to see a tree (or see one in your imagination). A tree needs light and water to survive. If it doesn't get enough of those things, its growth may be stunted. The tree won't grow as robust—it may become dry, brittle, and prone to breakage. When lightning strikes, that tree won't sustain as well. It's more likely to crack and splinter. It may even go up in flames.

For humans, mental blinders and emotional barriers can impede robust growth in a similar manner. If you don't address them, you may end up more brittle and less equipped to deal with the lightning strikes occurring in your daily life.

What do these mental blinders and emotional barriers look like? These are your unconscious habits and constructed preferences. Because the habits and preferences operate unconsciously, they blind you to your best growth conditions. They often are the source of plateau in your life. By perceiving human patterns through archetypes, especially your own, you can better perceive patterns of plateau that block living generatively and wholly.

Now, this requires some reflection. Reflection raises awareness and allows us to construct our own realities. It's straightforward. Nonetheless, most people don't bother to take the time for reflection, because they don't want to pause or they don't have the patience for it. In some cases, they aren't creating the conditions needed for reflection in their life; for example, they may avoid delineating boundaries that generate time for self.

I believe everybody has the capacity to be self-reflective. In fact, people usually don't *choose* to be reflective. This is largely because reflection can be uncomfortable. It can raise unsavory truths. The force of the emotional barrier to experience comfort is huge, so people tend to shy away from reflection.

Too often, this leads to regrets, sometimes combined with a feeling of longing. Take an example of someone who aspires to be an artist. Let's call him Pierre. Pierre might say, "I'm longing to be an artist, but I don't think I can make a living with it." Now, imagine Pierre is able to disconnect those two things: in truth, making a living and being an artist don't have to be tied together. It's possible for Pierre to be an artist in his choice of clothing, for instance. Pierre can be an artist in a class he takes on the weekends. He can be an artist and post his doodles on social media with no expectation of compensation, only with the desire to share his creations with the world.

This kind of dualistic thinking is a great example of how we get in a pattern of plateau. Pierre doesn't have to be an artist *or* make a living. He can be an artist *and* make a living doing something else. Art doesn't have to be his livelihood. The key is recognizing that that's what he wants and then breaking it down into smaller steps so that he isn't paralyzed with fear. This is exactly what coaching can do.

Have you ever fallen victim to dualistic thinking? Was there a time when you felt you were facing a "this or that" choice—without perhaps seeing the hidden third door of "this and that"? What might that have looked like?

EVOKE AWARENESS		
SOURCE	**MENTAL BLINDERS**	**EMOTIONAL BARRIERS**
Body	Dualistic thinking—Right and Wrong, Good and Bad	Control for Extreme Risk— Love / Loss
Heart	Comparison and competition	Comfort in Familiar—Suffer / Safe
Head	Expert status	FEAR / FOMO / FONI / FOPO*

*FEAR = False Evidence Appearing Real, FOMO = Fear of Missing Out, FONI = Fear of Not Being Important, FOPO = Fear of Other People's Opinions

Recognizing Patterns of Plateau

Our moments of reactivity reveal patterns. If we pay attention to those patterns, we may unveil emotional blinders and mental barriers. We can then start to identify patterns of plateau. However, sometimes those patterns of plateau are first revealed through symptoms.

Those symptoms of plateau fall into three central categories: mind, body, and heart. Exactly how those symptoms reveal themselves to us—or, rather, how we notice them—varies. As a coach, I'm oftentimes starting with symptoms of the head, because that's where the people I work with know where to start.

For example, I had a client who was in a cycle of obsessive reinvention. I'll call him Jason. Jason was noticing that his team was just not giving him what he wanted on a particular initiative, and he couldn't figure out why. He was super frustrated. We were sort of going around in circles as he was exploring the reason for this. We'd open one doorway, go in, and hit a wall.

It became clear that, while Jason was caught in this cycle of obsessive reinvention in his head, something else was going on. I said, "Let's push your chair back a couple inches." I wanted him to pull back for perspective and look at what was going on in his *whole* life, not just his work life.

It turned out that Jason had a daughter who was dealing with some serious health issues. I asked him, "Could this be about your daughter?" He started to get a little teary-eyed, and the emotion started welling up in him. It became clear that he had this whole emotional cycle of guilt and fear that was running in the background for him, even though he was trying to differentiate it from work. He was trying to partition it, but it wasn't working. It was too big.

So, Jason started experiencing these symptoms of plateau. Heart symptoms started showing, like surprising sadness about and doubt in his team. This wasn't really coming from the workplace. It was coming from his own guilt, worry, and fear around his daughter's illness. He was putting those doubts onto his team. At the same time, his symptoms of plateau were manifesting at the bodily level. He told me, "I'm not sleeping well." His body went into overdrive. Then, finally, his mental capacity started to diminish. He had a short fuse in meetings. He couldn't concentrate.

Jason and his family were dealing with issues that went beyond coaching, so he did go get support from a mental health professional. In fact, the whole family got support to navigate the situation. The illness of a child takes a toll on the whole group, siblings included. But it wasn't until Jason tried to examine his roadblocks at work that he realized how impactful the at-home situation was.

> Have you ever worked with a Jason, someone who seems stuck in a cycle of obsessive reinvention? Have you ever considered what might be causing that? Alternatively, have you ever felt the need to constantly reinvent the wheel, without being quite sure why?

SOURCE	PRESENCE OF PLATEAUS
Body	Self-sacrificing choices, addiction of any kind Quickly fatigued Poor sleeping
Heart	Doubt Annoyance—Prickly—Edgy Surprising sadness
Head	Obsessive reinvention Fuzzy logic Stalled decision-making

The Perspective from the Top of the Mountain

Dr. Paul Farmer was a wonderful man who dedicated much of his life to providing medical care in Haiti, one of the poorest countries in the world. Author Tracy Kidder wrote a book about Dr. Farmer's work, *Mountains beyond Mountains*, which gets its title from a Haitian proverb: "Beyond mountains, there are mountains." That's a useful phrase to keep in mind as you start to notice the things that are impeding your growth. As you pull back to see those patterns of plateau you've developed in your life, you'll start scaling mountains—but there will be more mountains.

Often, people get to the top of a mountain they imagined for themselves and say, "What else is there?" Or they completely ignore the fact that they're at the top of the mountain, and then they start protecting their newfound territory. Both cases become self-sabotage. The overindulgence of imagining that there is a permanent destination starts the process of the plateau.

Now, that's not to say it isn't useful to stop and celebrate. Of course, it is. But what do you celebrate? It's not having arrived at the destination. It's who you've become along the journey of getting to the destination. This is the key to continuous learning—what thinkers like American psychologist Dr. Carol S. Dweck call a growth mindset. In generative coaching work, the principle is to commit to the destination and then embrace the spontaneous journey.

That might sound daunting, like some never-ending journey. But remember, along the way, there are so many moments of bliss. Part of learning to perceive plateaus and patterns of reactivity also means learning to perceive those moments of bliss I mentioned in the introduction to this book. And that subtle shift in mindset will also relieve the effort of climbing the mountain.

You can tune your receptors to recognize things going on around you that you wouldn't have seen before, because you were too focused on the end game. You then tune into the experience as a whole. As a result, you'll be better equipped to *notice* the presence of tension; just as importantly, you'll be equipped to tolerate that tension—which is what we'll discuss next.

EXERCISE: CREATE YOUR TIMELINE

Pulling back for perspective sometimes means pulling *all* the way back and looking at your entire life, up until now. A common coaching exercise I use is the timeline.

Start by charting your life out in increments of five or ten years. So, if you choose to look at increments of five, you've got age five, ten, fifteen, twenty, and so on, all the way out. You might look at your life as a spiral (see next) that starts with your moment of birth at the center and opens out to the current moment.

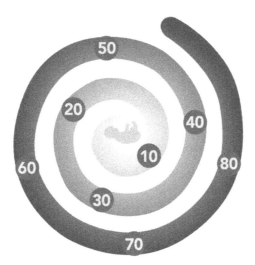

Ten years old

Twenty years old

Thirty years old

Forty years old

Fifty years old

Sixty years old

For each decade, write down the moments that shaped your mindset.

- What values did those moments instill in you?
- What guiding principles did you take away from them?
- What choices did those moments stimulate and you followed or didn't?

Take your own inventory throughout the decades. All of us have these moments, markers for the source of how we operate unconsciously got put into place.

Here's an example: I vividly remember when I was six years old, my brother was chasing me—we were playing football—and I fell down in our driveway and bumped my head. This was no small bump: we had one of those driveways with a steep drop off, so it was a drop of about ten feet. But I was fine. And I believe, even now, that this experience is part of where my attitude of "I can survive anything" comes from. It built a level of faith in my capacity, which contributed to some level of invulnerability. It's probably where my fearless intuition comes from.

Now, look at that inventory of things and ask yourself, *Are those still required now? If not, what do I choose instead?* For example, a person who grew up in an abusive household may be accustomed to keeping themselves small and staying quiet. As an adult, once they are in a safe space, these behaviors are arguably no longer necessary—but breaking them is often difficult.

Finally, consider what you're projecting out beyond another twenty or thirty years from whatever age you are today. Now, think about what inventory you need on the journey to that next destination.

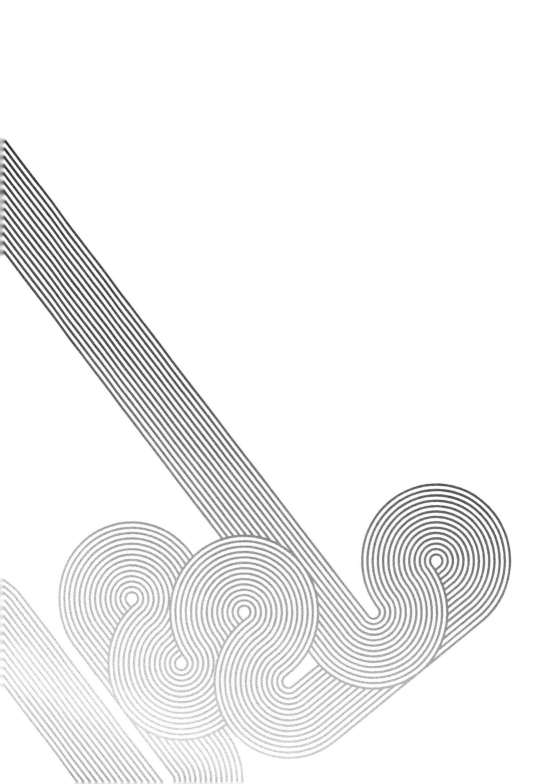

CHAPTER 4

TENSIONS OF PRESENCE IN LIFE

Problems are nothing but wake-up calls for creativity.
—GERHARD GSCHWANDTNER, FOUNDER AND
PUBLISHER OF *SELLING POWER* MAGAZINE

Plateaus are an indicator of a cycle. Throughout a human life, people go through patterns and cycle through stages of development. Cycles are part of the natural world we inhabit. Just look at the seasons. Look at animals, with their mating cycles. Look at plants, with their life cycles. Human beings, inhabiting the natural world, are not immune to cycles. And the presence of tension is a part of the human cycle.

Tension is a naturally occurring phenomenon. The problem is that, instead of treating it as such, we tend to treat it as a weakness or a threat—something to disavow or run from. What might happen if we allow ourselves to approach tension from a place of sovereignty, where we remind ourselves, *I have the power of choice, always*? When you operate from that inner authority, you can choose how you relate to the presence of tension, whatever it may be.

This starts with acknowledging that the tension is internal; it's not necessarily an external situation. You may *access* that tension through an exterior situation, but, even before that external trigger, that tension is already operating inside of you. You're holding both qualities inside of yourself at once. These qualities are both common in the human experience and unique to each context. Again and again, you need to pause and take time to identify the tensions and situate them in context.

In chapter 3, I have mentioned four general life tensions that are a basic part of being human: sovereignty and performance, intention and expectations, inside out and outside in, and relationship and person oriented versus process and plan oriented.

Beyond this, there are seven common tensions within us. We experience and dismiss these constantly. These tensions also tend to feed common leadership dilemmas—and I'll discuss how to deal with them from a leadership standpoint in greater detail in chapter 5. For now, I want to introduce these tensions and explore how we can use reflection to tolerate their presence and navigate them in productive ways.

The seven common tensions are as follows:

- Conflict and Breakthrough

- Conformity and Contribution

- Resistance and Risk-taking

- Entitlement and Self-responsibility

- Control and Agility

- Competition and Collaboration

- Apathy and Inspiration

TENSIONS OF PRESENCE

**Tolerate tension to find the right ratio for your
thorny problem and context**

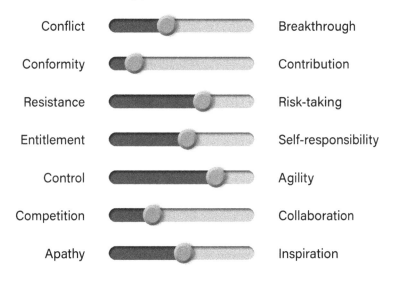

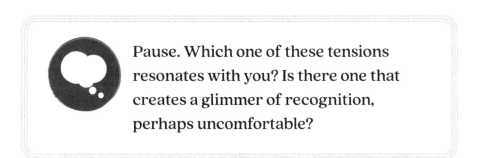

Pause. Which one of these tensions resonates with you? Is there one that creates a glimmer of recognition, perhaps uncomfortable?

You may not identify with any of these tensions immediately. That's because you probably don't even think about these tensions of presence, even as you experience them; you simply deflect. However, by deflecting these tensions, by failing to recognize them, you likely create behaviors that are unproductive, creating stress and anxiety internally—and placing stress on your external relationships, too.

Most of us externalize tension in this way. That includes you. You look for the cause of the tension, and you see that as the problem to solve. In fact, the tension you recognize is a symptom—one you're good at seeing externally but not so good at recognizing internally.

By the time plateaus appear, you're well beyond the point of recognizing the tension of presence. You've missed the opportunity to identify the tension, sit with it, reflect on it, and leverage it for generative change. In this chapter, I want to help you figure out how to catch that tension sooner and work with it productively. The way you do that is through the act of reflection, which allows you to recognize the system you're operating in, both internally and externally. That's also what the work of restoring your wholeness is about—being able to see what's actually your version of that tension that you hold in your worldview and mindset. We will look more closely at this in chapter 7 as part of deliberate judgment.

Recognizing Tension as a Tool for Finding Solutions

By embracing the idea that tension is always present, you can learn to recognize and work with it as a resource for finding solutions. The aim isn't to eliminate the pressure of the tension. It's about acknowledging it and then asking, *With that pressure, what's asking to be changed?* This is how you will begin to invite change. The tension appears because *something* wants to be different, but you don't know right off the bat what that is. It's not yet obvious; you simply feel the intention, the request, for change—through the presence of tension itself. The key to answering the question, to figuring out *what* wants to be different, requires pause.

It's not always easy to tolerate the presence of tension. However, if you take the time to sit in it and reflect on it, you can develop. You can break bad habits and release yourself from unproductive cycles. I know, because I've had to grapple with the presence of tension many times in my career. It has resulted in some painful sandpaper moments.

I am the kind of leader who will break things that are working in the name of ingenuity and innovation. That's not always a good thing. In the past, it's led to me being overly controlling. It took harsh feedback from a boss to illuminate this fact for me.

In 1992, my mother died of cancer on January 20, and my fiancé died of a heart attack on January 21. It was a shock to the system, to put it lightly. Shortly after, I took a four-month leave of absence. When I got back, my job wasn't there—or, it wouldn't be, soon. I had a few more months to cover me, but then I'd have to look for my next gig. I had a good amount of experience under my belt at that point, so I wasn't worried about finding something new—until I spoke to one of the executive leaders in another division. He told me, point-blank, "I would never hire you for an operational leadership position because people can't stand to work for you."

Ouch.

It was a gut punch. The tears started to flow. I took a couple of deep breaths to calm myself, and I looked at him and said, "In the ten years I've worked here, nobody has ever given me that feedback. Ever." I had never heard this, and I wanted clarity, so I asked him, "What are a couple of examples that you can give me to help me understand this?" Although he wasn't able to provide any examples (a classic "what not to do" in giving feedback), the impact was still there.

Despite the lack of examples, I knew that there had to be some truth to what he said—otherwise I wouldn't have had such a visceral reaction, full of emotion and physical feeling. My stomach twisted in a knot; the tears started flowing; my heart raced with anxiety. My body went into high alert—a great example of why you should always pay attention to those bodily reactions. My brain may have thought, *Come on, he doesn't even have examples! This feedback is nonsense!* but my body knew it better.

I started looking back over my ten-year tenure with the company, seeking answers. Trends began to emerge. I saw that I had always been given assignments doing really big, complex, innovative projects. So, I'd learned to innovate in an intuitive way. However, I often failed to explain the method to my madness to others on my team. My own emotional intelligence was out of sync. I was good at my work and enjoyed it. Professionally and personally, I was always pursuing those grand adventures I mentioned in the introduction to this book.

My full-steam-ahead approach meant I worked well with people who were confident, because I challenged them to do things that they never imagined they could do. However, I failed the people who needed a little more support; they became intimidated and were left unmoored, uncertain ships out at sea, while I powered ahead in my big boat. That was a leadership failure on my part.

When that executive told me, "I would never hire you for an operational leadership position because people can't stand to work for you," what he was flagging was my control. I was too controlling as a leader and not agile enough with diverse styles. I wasn't yet accommodating the fact that different people needed different things from me as a leader. Not only was I less accommodating, but I didn't even *see* those other styles or the need to be attentive to them, as well.

That gut-punch moment forced me to seriously reevaluate my leadership approach, my communication abilities, and the way I exerted control at work. *How could I be so blind?* That was the thought that cycled through my mind, again and again, and I really had to sit with the discomfort of that idea. How was it that I could have such a blank space around how I understood relating with colleagues and how colleagues were relating with me?

The tension—the gut punch of the tears, doubt, self-questioning—alerted me to the fact that *something had to change*. I took the time to figure out what. My solution? I started building teams and focusing on collaborative projects. There was a shift in me. I gave my team members more freedom and autonomy, and they started recognizing that I wasn't such a hard-ass after all; I was actually just a mush ball. I benefited, as did my team. Many of them grew and were promoted after that, while I went on to my next great adventure—better equipped to lead myself and those around me with compassionate honesty. It all began with a sandpaper moment—that tearful meeting in that executive's office. That was the first step to finding a solution.

Have you ever had this kind of sandpaper moment—feedback in the workplace that's come as a big surprise? It could be negative, as in my case, or it could be positive, something that someone else identified about you that was invisible to your own consciousness.

Tensions of Presence Are Not a Polarity or a Paradox

The tensions listed at the start of this topic may look like polar opposites, suggesting that you have to pick one or the other—inspiration or apathy, collaboration or competition, agility or control, and so on. This isn't the case. I've mentioned that I don't like to adhere to dualistic thinking, and this exemplifies why. If you go too far toward one end of the spectrum in these common tensions of presence, you're unlikely to achieve a satisfactory result. An example can help demonstrate what I mean.

I had a client, let's call him David, who was the chief operating officer for a long-standing family-owned business. This business had clear values dating back to its foundational roots. However, the board was five generations removed from the founder. They did not have the same values as that original founder. There may have been some overlap, but the context the company operated in—socially, historically, culturally—had changed dramatically. David's job was to protect the institution and its values while appeasing the board and keeping them content. Talk about walking a tightrope. As a result, David often found himself being the guardian of the mission, with the pressure of delivering the promise of the organization to its customers. It was an emotionally exhausting role.

This was exacerbated by the fact that David placed a huge premium on responsiveness. He was the kind of leader who was always available, always online. If he got an email in the middle of the night, from an overseas subsidiary, he'd respond at 7:01 the next morning, as soon as he opened his laptop. However, David also placed a premium on quality. He was a top-tier executive who crossed his t's and dotted his i's. Over time, those two values he held so dear started to create tension. This tension between responsiveness and quality became especially volatile as the board's values clashed with the company's fundamental values, and David found himself in the middle, trying to appease all sides and responding to all needs as fast as possible while still trying to uphold a certain level of quality.

There's the old saying, "You can have it fast, you can have it good, you can have it cheap: pick two." David wanted to do his job fast and good, but even that proved tricky. David was accustomed to thinking in black and white. He was by nature a dualistic thinker. If he drew up a contract, it was right or wrong. That's all there was to it.

To challenge David's naturally polarizing thinking, I had him do a somatic activity. Somatic activities use the mind-body connection to draw attention inward. They create awareness, allowing the individual to listen internally, which makes them useful for revealing what's often hidden deep in the mind and inaccessible to us on the surface. They're a wonderful coaching tool. In David's case, I hoped a somatic activity could help him gain clarity on his role within the company and illuminate how his values were informing that role.

I drew a line across the room. At one end, we put "quality" and, at the other end, "responsiveness." I had David stand in the middle of the line, between those two points, and I asked him how he thought about being responsive versus how he thought about quality. If he went all the way to the "quality" endpoint, what happened? If he went all the way to the "responsiveness" endpoint, what happened? (He literally moved to each end of the line as we talked this through—a somatic activity relies on *activity*.)

RESPONSIVENESS **QUALITY**

We started with responsiveness. David stood on that endpoint, and I said, "Put your legs right underneath you, feet underneath your hips, and get really comfortable. Keep your knees soft and really feel the gravity of your body in the earth. Take a few nice deep breaths. On each inhale, bring in the word responsiveness." I waited about thirty seconds until I could tell he was quiet with that moment. Then I asked him, "What are the benefits of the quality of responsiveness?" He said about half-a-dozen things, which I jotted down.

RESPONSIVENESS **QUALITY**

Next, I asked him, "What are the consequences when responsiveness is taken to an extreme? Take a few breaths and then just speak. Whatever comes, comes." He gave me some words, and I jotted them down.

Then I told him, "OK, shake that off. Now walk all the way over here to the other extreme."

So, he went to the quality endpoint. We repeated that exercise. I asked him, "What are the benefits?" and "What are the consequences if that gets taken to an extreme?"

RESPONSIVENESS   **QUALITY**

For David, one consequence appeared at both ends of the spectrum: inefficiency. Extreme quality and extreme responsiveness both had inefficiencies. When he realized that, his eyes just flew open and he was like, "Huh, I never thought about it that way." There was neither polarity nor paradox. It was clear that neither extreme was going to be satisfactory. There had to be some ratio between them.

I then had David stand in the middle of the line and said, "Let's start with 50:50. Put yourself right here. Open your legs a little bit more, like you're standing on the fulcrum of a teeter-totter. You can gently lean right or left. You can access all the way out to the edge of the extreme. From this place, what's available to you? What's possible if you're balancing quality and responsiveness?" In his response, some new ideas started to bubble up.

Then I asked, "As you think about the situation, does 50:50 ring true? Is that the right balance?" He said no—because there was risk associated with not having sufficient quality. I said, "OK, so what's the right ratio?" And he said, "I think it's 40:60—40 percent responsiveness and 60 percent quality." I asked why. His response: "There are some things on the quality side that cannot be compromised. We must manage expectations around when something will be completed to give priority to quality."

RESPONSIVENESS   **QUALITY**

That was the breakthrough moment. In talking—or, rather, moving—through it, David could see that different decisions had different risk profiles and thus needed different ratios of quality versus responsiveness. At the same time, he realized that he had never negotiated a key point with the board: managing expectations. In some cases, responsiveness could suffer, because the risk to the organization was too great if quality was compromised. However, his board was not thinking about the decisions he was bringing forward that way. This "ah-ha" moment was the first step toward finding a solution.

David ended up bringing an enterprise-risk model to the board to influence the dialogue about different initiatives—and they loved it. David was responsible for putting a whole new governance in place, a feather in his cap. The company now reports on enterprise risk every quarter using this model, and David no longer has the burden of serving as the "conscience" of the organization. He learned how to sit in the tension of quality versus responsiveness, and a new solution resulted.

 Can you relate to David's story? Are there times at work where you find yourself bumping against two extreme expectations—say punctuality versus perfection (let me remind you: there's no such thing as perfection), or being engaged versus preserving your personal energy, or speaking up versus letting others speak?

Reflection: The Key to Making the Most of Tension

I mentioned seven common tensions that tend to impact every human at one point or another. That list isn't exhaustive. My personal example above speaks most clearly to the tension between agility and control. However, there are also hints of other tensions there, such as contribution and conformity. I was so averse to the status quo, so in fear of conformity, I ran at a breakneck pace in the direction of contribution. But I overly contributed. I insisted on taking the lead when I should have been allowing others to exercise their skills and thoughts. This left less self-assured team members feeling undervalued and redundant—the last thing any leader who wants a motivated, thriving, and engaged team wants.

Tensions aren't mutually exclusive. Many can appear in more than one place or situation. This multiplicity makes the need for pause and reflection even greater.

In my case, through a process of reflection, I managed to sit in the tension of presence and recalibrate. I moved toward proactively building more collaborative teams and projects to counter my tendency toward hyper-control and excessively hands-on contribution. However, that kind of change isn't easy to achieve, and there are biological reasons for that.

There's a system in the body called the reticular activating system (RAS). A network of neurons located in the brain stem, the RAS, regulates what you filter out and what you allow to enter into your subconscious and conscious choices. It draws your attention toward what is meaningful or valuable, based on your former experiences. The human body sends some eleven million bits per second to the brain; however, the conscious mind is only able to process an estimated fifty bits per second.[12] So, the RAS exists to prioritize relevant information, or you'd be constantly overwhelmed.

Here's the catch: The brain prefers the familiar and prioritizes historical responses that were effective for you in the past. At the same time, it short-circuits your ability to perceive what's *new* in a given circumstance. Following habits is simply the more energy-efficient

---

12   *Encyclopedia Britannica*, 15th ed. (Britannica, 2012), s.v. "Physiology," https://www.britannica.com/science/information-theory/Physiology.

choice, but it's not necessarily the best choice given the current circumstances. For change to happen, you've got to override that biological instinct. How? Reflection is the answer.

Reflection is a source of solution because it heightens awareness.
It widens the camera lens on the territory that you're looking at. Or,
another favorite metaphor of mine: it gives you a wider look through
the front windshield of your car, so you're no longer relying solely on
your tiny rearview mirror.

In the first chapter, I noted that reflection must be active, whereas
it's often understood as passive. Breaking down the skill of reflection
into its smaller micro-skills can help clarify it as a process:

1. The first micro-skill requires *seeing that a situation is worthy of
    pausing* and giving it enough time. This requires recognizing
    the long-term value of pause.

2. The second micro-skill requires *noticing all that's occurring*.
    Recognize what's arising from the unconscious, learned, and
    adopted habits and preferences that don't fit the situation
    very well.

3. The third micro-skill requires patience for *staying with the
    question*. You've got to stay with a question about motiva-
    tion long enough to let it really percolate. There's always
    going to be more than one answer. You can't just turn the
    heat up and let the water simmer. You've got to give it time
    to come to boil so that you can fully explore those varied
    elements that shaped the choices made, actions taken, and
    results produced.

The micro-skills of reflection fuel the first step in the vehicle for
generative change—a car or, in this case, ACAAR.

ACAAR: Your Vehicle for Generative Change

If we attune ourselves to notice the presence of tension sooner, we can catch it before undesirable outcomes—such as plateau—occur. Wonder is how we tolerate that tension, adopting that rapt state of attentiveness and astonishment at something new. This is what allows us to ask and explore that *What needs to change?* question—the question that often arises after a gut-punch moment.

The word "wonder" has some childlike or whimsical connotations in Western culture and is often replaced with the word "curiosity," which is not quite the same. Even curiosity has some scary implications—curiosity killed the cat, right? But the definition of curiosity itself is simply "an eager wish to know or learn something."[13] That's it.

That's how I suggest approaching tension: let it inspire your rapt attention and astonishment that something new can and will emerge from the choice to pause, notice, and reflect. Your moments of tension are telling you something. It's up to you to reflect and figure out what.

Again, reflection is like a muscle that you need to build. If you strengthen that muscle, the elapsed time between the situation that generates tension and your recognition of that situation as a trigger point will shrink. Your body is an instrument that you can finely tune to those moments. When a disruption occurs, interrupting the ease and flow of daily being, people often ignore the early signs, but that's not tolerating tension, and that's surviving in the midst of the tension. You want to tune your instrument to pick up the signs early.

---

13   *Cambridge Advanced Learner's Dictionary*, 4th ed. (Cambridge: Cambridge University Press, 2013), s.v. "Curiosity," https://dictionary.cambridge.org/dictionary/english/curiosity.

This begins with pausing to examine the unsatisfactory results—asking yourself *what happened*. The vehicle for generative change is, in fact, a vehicle—a car, or ACAAR, the "R" standing for results, which is your starting point. ACAAR provides a way to deconstruct tension. Instead of focusing on *symptoms* (think my tears in the afore-mentioned meeting), you're forced to focus on the issue.

Process improvement methodology is a testament to this fact of life: the entire Six Sigma Lean body of work posits that, if you want to get very effective at process improvement, you have to look beyond symptoms. Where do you start? You start with the thing you didn't like. Often, that comes in the form of external feedback, as was the case for me. Ultimately, you begin with the result you didn't find satisfying or, worse yet, overwhelmingly negative, and impactful.

Results -> Actions -> BEFORE
Alignment -> Clarity -> Facilitate Awareness

Here's what ACAAR looks like:

- *Results.* It starts with asking, *What happened?* The unsatisfactory result needs to be articulated in great detail.

  - What made the situation unsatisfactory?

  - What made it create a ripple impact or enact some kind of negative influence?

  - How long did it take before this was caught?

  - What measures were being used?

  ▫ What measures were lagging?

- *Actions. What were the actions taken to produce the unsatisfactory result?* In this step you're getting beyond symptoms and getting into clearer problem definition.

  ▫ Who took what actions?

  ▫ At what stage of process or project did those actions occur?

  ▫ In what scope did the team pursue those actions?

- *Alignment. What was the basis of the decision?*

  ▫ What were the beliefs you had? This would be your habit preference, assumption, or bias.

  ▫ What made you think that those beliefs were the right criteria from which to decide what actions to take?

- *Clarity. What actions were faulty (as in, they did not produce the desired result)?* Such actions could cover all kinds of things.

  ▫ How much money was spent?

  ▫ How many people were deployed?

  ▫ What were the qualities and traits and experience of those people?

  ▫ What timelines were established?

  ▫ What stakeholders were involved in decision-making?

- *Awareness. What data were you looking at that initiated the process or project?*

  ▫ What was the source of the data?

  ▫ What was the veracity of that data?

□ What might you have dismissed or disregarded and now see that as a mistake?

Leaders, in particular, can use ACAAR to navigate thorny situations in the workplace and develop new solutions. Starting in chapter 5, I'll look more concretely at how leaders can harness newfound awareness and clarity to tolerate the presence of tension and use it for greater alignment, deliberate action, and desirable results. To make this as tangible as possible, I'll explore the seven common leadership dilemmas. The tensions of presence described previously tend to manifest in these dilemmas, again and again, in the workplace. As a leader, understanding these tensions and how to approach them is invaluable.

EXERCISE: PRACTICE INHABITING TENSION

In this chapter, I described a somatic exercise I did with my client, David. This is an exercise I frequently do with clients, and it's something you can do on your own—no in-person coach needed.

The next time you notice the presence of tension—be it one of the tensions listed in this chapter or another one altogether—try this exercise. I'll use the tension of "entitlement" and "self-responsibility" to make this example more tangible.

VISUALIZE AN IMAGINARY LINE ON YOUR FLOOR
Explore the qualities on either side:

Entitlement | Self-Responsibility

Walk the Line: Experience the Extremes and Middle Balance

1. Draw an imaginary line on the floor. At one end, place the quality of entitlement. At the other end, place the quality of self-responsibility (or whatever qualities you are navigating).

2. Go to the endpoint *entitlement*. Ask yourself, *What are the benefits of the quality of entitlement?* Jot down your answers.

3. Remaining on the endpoint *entitlement*, ask yourself, *What are the consequences when entitlement is taken to an extreme?* Jot down your answers.

4. Go to the endpoint *self-responsibility*. Ask yourself, *What are the benefits of the quality of self-responsibility?* Jot down your answers.

5. Remaining on the endpoint *self-responsibility*, ask yourself, *What are the consequences when self-responsibility is taken to an extreme?* Jot down your answers.

6. Look for points of overlap. Are there any? Capture these.

7. Now, start moving along your invisible line. Consider the implications of various ratios of self-responsibility versus entitlement in diverse scenarios. Find that sweet spot. What ratio fits what purpose? You'll likely have more than one answer.

8. Now, what do you need to achieve that ratio? For example, in David's case, it meant managing expectations, both his own and those of external parties (the board). What do *you* need to achieve *your* sweet spot, the appropriate ratio?

You now have points that you can use to start to build an action plan. For example, in David's case, this meant bringing an enterprise-risk model to his board. What does your action plan look like?

You've walked the tightrope of tension and taken the first steps, quite literally, in finding a possible solution.

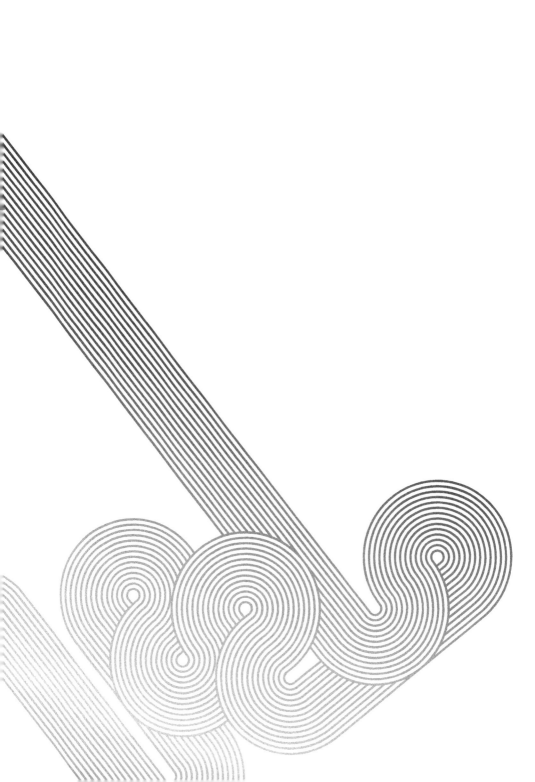

CHAPTER 5
SEVEN COMMON LEADER DILEMMAS

It's better to solve a problem five different ways,
than to solve five problems one way.
—GEORGE PÓLYA, MATHEMATICIAN

A t the beginning of chapter 4, I have discussed the fact that humans are not immune to cycles—such as the presence of plateaus. Every person has their own cycles of growth and development. However, these cycles don't happen in a vacuum. Cycles interconnect and intertwine, and your recognition and understanding of those cycles change over time as your life context evolves. Again, we can look to nature for inspiration.

Consider something as basic as the food chain. The life cycle of a plant impacts the life cycle of a small herbivore, which impacts the life cycle of a larger carnivore or omnivore—which impacts the life cycle of an even *bigger* carnivore or omnivore. There are plenty of real-world examples of how disrupting one part of an ecosystem disrupts others. For instance, when destructive fishing practices and poor water quality decimate seagrass meadows, a vital habitat and food source for many marine animals disappears.

Now, think of humans. Imagine all those humans, with all their cycles, in an interconnected environment—like a workplace. The tensions that will arise are inevitable. In the worst-case scenarios, those tensions can lead to organizational breakdowns. As a leader, it's often your job to navigate these tensions and, ideally, prevent breakdown.

The tensions of presence mentioned in chapter 4 lend themselves to seven common leadership dilemmas, which I'll delve into later. These dilemmas came from a survey of some 250 leaders my organization did—I mentioned it briefly in the introduction. The survey was given to leaders from director to C-suite level, as well as a few board-level leaders. Individuals surveyed were distributed across a range of industries. My organization largely works with people in manufacturing, technology, healthcare, financial services, and hospitality, but we also work with people beyond those fields.

The aim of the survey was to figure out *what* was standing in the way of leaders being generative. At that time, it was already clear to us that being generative was a way for leaders to sustain excellence. The next logical question was, how could we nurture that generative state? So, we asked the leaders directly: "What things are getting in the way of your learning to be a generative leader?"

We started to see these seven common dilemmas show up. There were some synonym words—the verbiage wasn't always identical, but the trends were clear. Also striking was the fact that the leaders we surveyed complained that they could never find a way to *get rid of* these dilemmas; they just had to live with them. We found this language very telling, and it helped evolve our approach.

The question no longer became "How do we avoid tension?" but "How do we learn to tolerate the discomfort of tension, something that never goes away and is always present in varying degrees? How do we start to befriend it?" That's what this book is about. None of this is about *eliminating* the tension. The tension just is.

Tension is inevitable and natural—especially in an increasingly complex world informed by accelerating change. There's always more than one right answer, especially in the ubiquitous complexity of today's world. In the modern world, we are presented with mounds of information; it's unreasonable to expect one person to sift through it all and come up with the right answer or innovative idea on their own.

> The question no longer became "How do we avoid tension?" but "How do we learn to tolerate the discomfort of tension?"

By accepting tension as a natural thing, we can get away from fearing it and instead embrace our curiosity, working better with others to learn the many facets of any given situation. This is how good decision-making gets done, by seeing all angles. Do you have all the angles yourself? Probably not. Through patience, you slow down the response to problem-solving and start to recognize where to channel your curiosity, with whom, in what context, and for what contribution.

At the same time, inviting these other perspectives is what allows you to help break free of the limitations of polarity and paradox. When we hold something as a polarity, we immediately get caught in the dualistic thinking, the prevailing approach. Paradox is slightly more complex, because in paradox, two things can coexist.

As individuals, it's easy to fall into the trap of polarity or paradox, which can make navigating the complexity of the world more difficult—we see it in black and white, without consideration for the many shades between. For individuals, this leaves limited leeway. As a team, it's easier to find those shades between. But it starts with the leader pressing pause.

Why You, the Leader, Must Press Pause

As a leader, whatever decision you're making isn't only influencing you—it's also influencing other stakeholders. That could include anyone from employees to customers. The thorniness of a leadership dilemma tends to grow as the complexity of stakeholders grows. Will your decision impact ten people or ten thousand? Each person has their own stake in the decisions getting made and their own experiences being produced from those decisions.

The complexity of the system alone should encourage leaders to pause. Ironically, it's precisely when big decisions need to be made that leaders often face pressure to act quickly and decisively. However, moving quickly can have unintended consequences that are difficult to recover from.

Pause.

Consider all the stakeholders your decision may impact. This starts with examining your own mind—your habits, preferences, assumptions, and biases. That's step one.

Step two is considering the mindset of the other stakeholders involved. It's asking yourself, *I wonder if this person is operating out of the same set of habits, preferences, assumptions, and biases as I am?* Probably not. It then begs the question: *What mindset are they operating from?*

This is a moment where you allow wonder to bubble up. As the other person's mindset comes to light, you might find yourself in a state of shock or astonishment, like *Woah, I had no idea that this was where they were coming from! No wonder we ended up taking the steps we did.* Only then can you begin to identify the actions that created whatever unsatisfactory result you're grappling with.

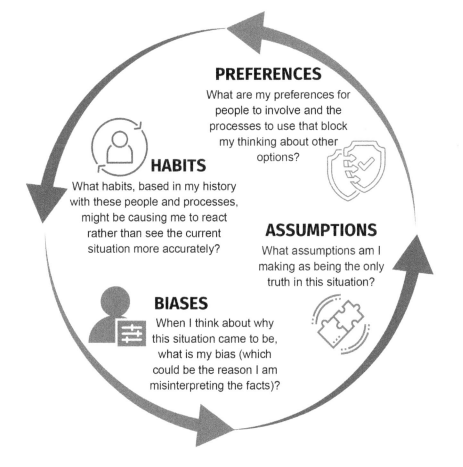

PREFERENCES
What are my preferences for people to involve and the processes to use that block my thinking about other options?

HABITS
What habits, based in my history with these people and processes, might be causing me to react rather than see the current situation more accurately?

ASSUMPTIONS
What assumptions am I making as being the only truth in this situation?

BIASES
When I think about why this situation came to be, what is my bias (which could be the reason I am misinterpreting the facts)?

One timely example of this is the great "back to the office" debate. During the COVID-19 pandemic, many companies transitioned to a work-from-home model. Now, as the pandemic becomes smaller and smaller in the rearview mirror, some are desperately trying to get their workers back into the office. In many cases, the schism is producing disastrous outcomes in terms of employer–employee relationships.

A CEO of a media company, I'll call her Driana, was adamant about people returning to the office five days a week. Driana was ready to die on this hill. She was determined to get people back into the building and told everyone who would listen that the culture was in grave risk of changing, unintentionally and in ways she didn't want.

Others in Driana's leadership team issued a warning. They told her, "You cannot do this. Our workforce will not come back five days a week, and you will find yourself without a workforce." For some time, an ugly battle raged. Eventually, Driana backed down from her demands for a no-exceptions return to the office.

This situation could have gone very differently. A number of companies have already experienced the fallout of calling workers back to the office, only to discover that they aren't coming back—even if that means quitting.[14] In the cases of those workers who do come back, research suggests they're "quiet quitting" and no longer engaged at work.[15] Luckily, in Driana's case, there was space created for pause—and that pause allowed for dialogue within the leadership team. But there was a period of palpable tension first.

Even if the tension isn't as obvious as in Driana's case, even if it's just simmering below the surface, it can still be present—and these situations can be even more damaging. This distinctly felt yet invisible tension festers. Over time, it becomes destructive leadership

---

14   Bryan Lufkin, "The Workers Quitting over Return-to-Office
      Policies," BBC, May 24, 2022, https://www.bbc.com/worklife/
      article/20220523-the-workers-quitting-over-return-to-office-policies.

15   "State of the Global Workplace: 2023 Report," Gallup, 2023, https://www.gallup.com/
      workplace/349484/state-of-the-global-workplace.aspx.

and acceptable incivility, negatively impacting both retention and attraction. Just glance at Glassdoor to see how easy it is to damage a company's reputation in the minds of prospective personnel.

> Have you ever had an "I will die on this hill!" moment at work? How did it play out? Alternatively, have you ever had to negotiate with someone taking such a hard-line stance—a Driana of your own? What was the outcome?

The key to avoid that kind of distinctly felt simmering tension comes through improving your noticing muscle—*learning to* notice, which I have talked about in chapter 2. Then, the trick to navigating any tension comes from sitting with the tension a little longer. You must sit in that uncomfortable state until you see a recombination of both sides, by practicing wonder and looking more closely at what motivates the rise of the tension. Let's look at how that can be put into practice in the context of the seven common leadership dilemmas.

Seven Common Leadership Dilemmas

Already, we are seeing an increase in thorny issues in the workplace. From intergenerational pressures to technological pressures (hello, generative artificial intelligence [AI]), there are many factors at play. Every leader that I've engaged suspects that issues in the workplace will only continue to become thornier. This makes it all the more imperative that leaders learn to pause and sit in tension. There are seven common leadership tensions that executives refer to as dilemmas seeking a solution.

However, as introduced in the previous chapter, the dilemmas are qualities of tension—symptoms and not root causes of breakdowns.

Leaders start with the dilemma, and they find better answers by attending to it. It's not as simple as moving from one state to another state, because the thing you're moving from doesn't go away. It's an internal tension. What you want is to recognize what it represents. For example, when conflict arises, it represents a failure to communicate sufficiently—or, when resistance shows up, it's an indicator that people require reassurance.

Accept that the presence of tension can inform you about what's *really* occurring. Tension then becomes an important way to calibrate the way that you show up and interact with people.

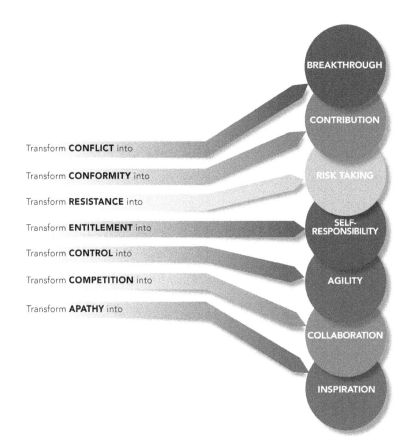

Transform **CONFLICT** into — BREAKTHROUGH

Transform **CONFORMITY** into — CONTRIBUTION

Transform **RESISTANCE** into — RISK TAKING

Transform **ENTITLEMENT** into — SELF-RESPONSIBILITY

Transform **CONTROL** into — AGILITY

Transform **COMPETITION** into — COLLABORATION

Transform **APATHY** into — INSPIRATION

Now you're going to see the transformation from dilemma to tension of presence and how you can use this to empower yourself to engage in the reflection process. Before you dive in, a caveat: beware that you will be predisposed to identify these qualities as "desirable" versus "undesirable," or "good" versus "bad." This is human nature and speaks to the dualistic thinking we naturally pursue. However, remember, this isn't a question of polarities or picking one or the other. Think back to David's example: it wasn't by embracing one endpoint or the other that he found success. Rather, it was about finding the right ratio. Further, that ratio will change depending on the context.

For each of the dilemmas mentioned next, you'll find some bullet points to help you hold the tension and shift your mindset. Keep that idea of the ratio in mind as you proceed through these dilemmas. Remember, it isn't about going 100 percent one way or the other. It's about holding the tension and finding the right balance for the specific situation.

HOLD THE TENSION OF CONFLICT AND BREAKTHROUGH

Conflict is one example of interference with workplace performance that leaders navigate daily. Many leaders witness stressful conflict in the workplace and then get stressed out trying to figure out what to do about it. Unfortunately, seeking quick relief from any tension often amplifies the problem, because rapid action relies on incomplete information. The alternative to quick relief arises when you negotiate—and compromise—to get something useful.

Say you're dealing with two employees bickering in the workplace. Your initial thought may be, *I want these people to stop arguing with each other and pay attention to the job that needs to get done.* You're eager to go from conflict to breakthrough. However, the seeds of the conflict can also be the source of your breakthrough—if you take the time to examine them. Examples where I frequently see this are the problems of market share or customer retention. These hot-button topics often lead to disagreements on how to fix them; different teams may have different takes. Customer service says this, while sales says that, and marketing says something else entirely. The solution often lies within the disagreement. A generative leader will explore all possibilities to find it.

Take a second to pause. Think of a time when you didn't hold the tension of conflict and breakthrough long enough. For instance, maybe a problem reared its ugly head and—in an attempt to put it to bed quickly—you fired off an email response without completely understanding what was occurring.

Consider these three ideas to help hold the tension as you move between conflict and breakthrough:

1. **Remember, we all want to feel like we belong.** People don't come to work wanting to create conflict and have a bad day. As human beings, we want to feel like we belong and enjoy our time in the workplace. Responsibility to create an enjoyable workplace climate begins with each leader. By recognizing that employees didn't come to work to create conflict, you're taking a step toward wonder. Start by asking questions to learn about what is generating the attitude you observe in others.

2. **Guard against conflict.** Step two is more about how you can guard against conflict. This step focuses on respect—giving it to get it in return. Pause for a moment to recall the last time you were in a conversation with someone who was unkind toward you. You could probably feel stress and a sense of conflict arising in your awareness. Imagine if you'd said, "Can you pause for a minute? Let's have a conversation about what's going on here." That takes emotional courage, even for an experienced leader. Now, imagine your employees don't know how to do that. If you don't model it, they won't learn to. It's your job to find out what's going on for people before concluding that the person(s) is/are somehow the cause of the conflict.

3. **Listen and notice differently.** Remember this: when you embody a mindset that everybody in the workplace has everything necessary to be at their best all the time, you listen differently. You *notice* differently. This makes you more likely to find opportunities to move from a "telling" style of leading to one that is more about shared responsibility, empowerment, and learning. You may realize, *I bet this person in front of me has an idea to resolve this conflict on their own.* You don't have to do it for them. Ask, "What do you see as a possible resolution for this conflict?"

HOLD THE TENSION OF CONFORMITY AND CONTRIBUTION

Conformity was the norm in the industrial age and, in many ways, carried the seed of today's emphasis on lean and agile principles. By eliminating variability, employee conformity saves money, improves productivity, and generates growth more quickly. Unfortunately, this creates an unintended consequence that everyone struggles with today—unique contribution gets squashed. When a team member chooses conformity, because that provides both emotional and economic security, the enterprise does not have access to that person's unique contributions.

As I entered the workforce in the '70s, I often heard that it was best not to "rock the boat." Well, it's not the '70s anymore. "Disruptive innovation" has become a buzzword and a holy grail. It's recognized that extreme conformity can lead to tension. Consider a customer service role: a customer wants to return a product, and the sales associate says, "That's not our policy. I can't take it back. It's in the rules." That means an unhappy customer. If that sales associate was empowered to question the rules, that didn't have to happen.

 Pause for a moment and reflect on how you perceive your workplace. Do employees play it safe, keeping their heads down and mouths shut, doing the work? Do they stay silent, conforming to the status quo, instead of sharing ideas and innovation? Might you be a leader longing for more engagement and contribution from an employee or your team?

Consider these three ideas to help hold the tension as you move between conformity and contribution:

1. **Be alert for your autopilot mindset.** Reflect on your current habits, thoughts, beliefs, values, attitudes, and frames of reference. They are part of your autopilot mindset and guide

your daily work. The first step of noticing makes you curious about what motivates your choice of action and interaction. You can then consider what's more practical for the current environment, situation, or relationship. Now, your personal patterns can become clearer to recognize along with the impact those patterns generate. Use these questions to invite change in your rhythm so that you can be more deliberate with your desired impact:

- What are the ways that you conform to that work for you and your role?

- What are some ways you conform to that no longer work for you and your role?

- What is the new road that you want to take?

- What are the talents and strengths you've developed, and how can you contribute those to carry you forward into the next role you desire?

2. **Learn about others' mindsets.** After the above reflection, you may realize that you don't fully know your team members beyond what they do on the job. This means you also don't know their mindset—their own autopilot that operates invisibly within them. Explore the questions with each team member in a one-on-one. Give attention toward play, purpose, and potential, bringing team members together to share more about themselves and get to know each other beyond their roles. By this action, you, as their leader, signal your interest, support, and respect for each person's unique presence on the team. Leaders who adopt these behaviors

satisfy what Dr. Timothy R. Clark defines as the first stage of psychological safety, Inclusion Safety.

3. **Create psychological safety.** Would you like the key to stimulating new ideas and solutions from your team, to fully engage them? Remember that it requires bravery for a team member to choose to step out from conformity and be different. Leaders who sustain this understanding create psychological safety. When team members feel unsafe expressing their unique capability to make a meaningful contribution, ingenuity, productivity, and improvement stall. As a leader, you want to achieve a stage well beyond inclusion: Dr. Clark's "Challenger Safety" motivates team members to speak up and challenge the status quo when they notice an opportunity to improve.

> **When team members feel unsafe expressing their unique capability to make a meaningful contribution, ingenuity, productivity, and improvement stall.**

HOLD THE TENSION OF RESISTANCE AND RISK-TAKING

Leaders in the workplace face all kinds of resistance. Resistance from others generates internal resistance that festers, putting the brakes on the risk-taking that's required to engage with constant change. Leaders may also face their own resistance. That said, resistance isn't always bad; it can be healthy. Your resistance suggests that what you've been doing so far has been comfortable and stabilizing. It's a classic rubber-band scenario—figuring out how far to stretch the band without snapping it.

In those scenarios, if you move to resistance too fast, you fail to reflect on what risk-taking contributes: what is perceived as reckless and damaging may, in fact, be innovative and useful. There's some ratio between the two that works. When you can physically stand somewhere between resistance and risk-taking—as in that somatic exercise at the end of chapter 4—and sense what's useful and what's not, you'll be able to make better decisions. As you shift your mindset, you can think about resources differently. A more deliberate decision-making process nurtures curiosity and solutions.

 Pause. You've surely felt the tension of being asked to change and take a risk on something unknown. Think of that moment now. You might have liked the end idea associated with the risk but weren't confident about the outcome that would result from moving forward. What did you end up doing? Did you take a big leap? Was it a case of paralysis by analysis? Did you make a small hop instead?

Consider these three ideas to help hold the tension as you move between resistance and risk-taking:

1. **Be curious versus reactive.** What do you do with a direct report that shows signs of resistance? They may appear withdrawn, respond defensively to feedback, or appear to do only the bare minimum. Remember, the responsibility to create an enjoyable workplace climate begins with each

leader. Instead of getting annoyed, take a moment to pause—and get curious. What could be causing the resistance you see this person exhibit? The most important thing you can do to find out is to create an atmosphere of trust. What does it take to build trust? You can listen instead of telling them. You can invite their insights rather than instructing based on your knowledge. You can create a space where they feel they can say what matters to them.

2. **Create opportunities for development.** The second idea focuses on shifting from a performance to a developmental mindset. Performance is essential in any organization. Obviously, you have to focus on output and accomplishments. However, it's critical to look beyond outcomes and consider what's going on for people around their work. Focusing on the person rather than the position will help them shift from a resistant mindset to an open and risk-taking mindset. You might ask them questions like:

   - "What matters to you most about your work?"

   - "What challenges do you feel are in your way to bring your best self to work each day?"

   - "What hurdles interfere with your ability to use your competence and authority?"

   - "What can I do to remove those hurdles and give you more autonomy?"

   These questions communicate to your associates and colleagues at any level that you care about them as individuals, not just for their output.

3. **Learn fast versus fail fast inspires.** Remember this: everybody will misstep. Focus on learning instead of shaming and blaming. Otherwise, the risk is that people will go into protective mode, which squashes passion and creativity. As a leader, it's your job to help your associates shift from a mindset that focuses on the fear of failing to one that recognizes the invitation to learning. That's what's behind the whole idea of generativity and generative coaching. We can learn and grow from all the experiences we are having. Embodying this mindset as a leader allows your associates and direct reports to move from a closed mindset to a creative space. The result? A greater willingness to take risks.

HOLD THE TENSION OF ENTITLEMENT AND SELF-RESPONSIBILITY

Like many leaders, you may be wondering how we arrived at this moment in society (and in workplaces) where people perceive others as walking around as if they're the only one that matters. There seems to be a broad consensus that modern people are a bit self-absorbed and unconcerned about how others experience life. As a leader, you want self-responsibility in the workplace; you expect everyone to act appropriately without great explanation. However, you're confronted with entitlement. Please, remove the negative connotation of that word, "entitlement," and look at it as the dictionary defines it: "something that you have a right to do or have, or the right to do or have something."[16]

The tension between entitlement and self-responsibility has become more acute as most companies simultaneously experience five

---

16   *Cambridge Advanced Learner's Dictionary*, 4th ed. (Cambridge: Cambridge University Press, 2013), s.v. "Entitlement," https://dictionary.cambridge.org/dictionary/english/entitlement.

generations in the workplace. We're finding that older generations, Gen X and the boomers who remain, tend to look at the younger generations as entitled. Why? One reason I've been given is that they always ask for feedback. Why are they asking for feedback? Because the system doesn't give them any. They have no idea what the hell they're doing. However, their leaders don't realize that they're not very good at delegating. They don't close the feedback loop to say, "Hey, when you did X, it produced Y. Good job." They just say, "Good job." Good job for what? It feels disingenuous. Realistically, if you want workers to take self-responsibility, you, the leader, must recognize that they are entitled to feedback. Further, by providing specific, timely, and relevant feedback about the behaviors an employee embodied that created success, you can generate commitment and a sense of belonging. Those sensory experiences intrinsically motivate employee engagement, encouraging individuals to use their discretionary energy enthusiastically.

Pause. When is the last time an employee asked you for feedback? How did you respond? What course of action did you take? Did you commit to giving them a comprehensive, thoughtful report—or was it more cursory? Alternatively, have you ever asked for feedback, only to be underwhelmed by the response?

Consider these three ideas to help hold the tension as you move between entitlement and self-responsibility:

1. **Be present.** I know you've heard this before. What matters here is not that you understand the two words, *be present.* Instead, consider what keeps you from being present and how that's causing the breakdown—negatively charged entitlement showing up in people rather than them taking self-responsibility. Think about the last time your boss was really present with you. What was your reaction to it? What about a time you noticed their absence of presence? What was your reaction to it? The absence of presence has an impact on us because we make assumptions about whether we are worthy, important, or valued. What is preventing your presence?

2. **Pay attention to your impact.** The step to building and sustaining your muscle to *be present* arises from noticing what happens when you are not. Tap into your motivation for high engagement, and do your part by modeling that experience with yourself. Choose to notice distractions from what's important—and pause. Even a split-second pause breaks the habit for that moment and affords an opportunity to consider a different choice. With the habit broken, you can choose to shift attention to being present with what's right in front of you. By the way, it's OK to be distracted, and that's normal, especially in our modern, chaotic world! Noticing and shifting back to presence becomes the muscle you want toned up.

3. **Demonstrate your curiosity that invites others.** Finally, exercise your natural curiosity. Curiosity about how another person perceives and makes meaning of a situation always produces more effective action. Allow curiosity to live in your mindset so that, in listening, you begin to hear the gem, the

sparkle, the inner motivation for the other person's choices. It could be one little idea they mention where you realize, "Oh, if they pursued that idea, that would make a big difference." Ask about it. Extend an invitation to share. This helps you learn to see the person beyond your assumptions and biases.

HOLD THE TENSION OF CONTROL AND AGILITY

This is an interesting one for leaders, because many desire control and agility in extremes. You may recognize this in yourself. You want to keep tight control of what's going on around you while also wanting to move quickly. The truth is that you need both. Control provides a baseline, affirming the fundamental principles that keep your organization intact. However, agility is needed to recognize when a best practice is no longer a best practice.

Six Sigma and Lean process improvements are an interesting example. They're all about learning to fail *quickly*. Taking this model to the extreme, modern software companies are increasingly cutting in-house testing and simply using continuous release. Instead of alpha and beta testing, they just put a product on the market. Their consumers tell them quickly what needs fixing—and the company fixes it (sometimes at the expense of their reputation). Now, instead of failing fast, wouldn't it be better to *learn* fast—to look at the full set of data and consider what might have been discounted or dismissed in some way? That's another level of discernment that can arise when you envision creating a customer experience that represents an effective ratio of control and agility. For the highly competitive software market, continuous release delivers consistent quality and anticipates the influence of external events that require an agile response.

Pause. Now get ready to be honest with yourself—really honest. Have you ever micromanaged a project, team, or employee? I am sure there was some reason for it; maybe you were putting out a metaphorical fire, or there was some major consequence, like an end-of-year figure, on the line. But now wonder, Was there a different way than the one you took?

Consider these three ideas to embody the balance between control and agility that is appropriate to your context:

1. **Notice voids and build context to understand.** Are the messages you are sending being received as you intended? Pay attention to how others respond to you in conversation—their energy, attitude, language, and pace. Now switch places. When you show up in only partial presence, you're not getting the messages your employees intend to send to you. While you think you're controlling the chaos around you and getting stuff done, you're creating an unintended consequence: your employees feel that they're left in the dark. They think that you don't trust them; what's more, they think that you don't respect their thinking. Partial engagement doesn't do it. You need to stop and pause what you're doing to receive the message entirely and to allow the messages you deliver to be fully received before marching forward. That pause leads to an open exchange and allows you to deliberately offer and receive open attention.

2. **Choose to express optimistic thinking.** When you create a trusting, respectful environment, you're embodying optimistic thinking. In other words, imagine a meeting where you showed up and said something like, "OK, what's the return-to-green plan here? Why do we have so many things in yellow and red?" Imagine if you'd started the meeting a little differently and said, "Let's acknowledge the things that are in green right now. I want to hear what everyone here is most proud of in our progress." And then say, "Given that success, what could we apply to the things in yellow and red?" And then, "What can I contribute to help you get through the things in yellow and red, and return those to green?" Adopting and expressing optimism elevate your faith in the team's resourceful, capable, and creative wholeness. In their minds, they will receive this as a simple but powerful message: *I believe in you.*

3. **Practice pause to exercise valuable curiosity.** The minute you think you need to jump into a conversation, actively exercise pause in some way. You might soften your gaze, take a breath, or smile. Alternatively, you might push your chair back an inch or two. Whatever form your pause takes, the purpose is to short-circuit your habit of jumping in and rescuing, having the idea, or anticipating what others might want from you. Ask a question instead, particularly one you don't know the answer to and couldn't possibly understand because that answer lives inside the other person. By asking, you show them that you most definitely want to learn what they think. The first skill for valuable curiosity? Pause. With diligent practice, you'll see people change around you. They will come to realize that your confidence means they have

permission to be agile. Meanwhile, you get out of the controlling-the-chaos business.

HOLD THE TENSION OF COMPETITION AND COLLABORATION

You've reached some level of leadership, thanks in part to some sort of technical expertise you have. You have a point of view informed by lived experience and learned knowledge. In leadership, issues may arise when this expertise is seen as a know-it-all attitude, which can undermine collaboration. You may also see these instances in others in your organization. I described Ricardo, in the second chapter—his expertise was there, but it was standing in the way of his partnering and, in the big picture, his professional advancement. He was creating an environment of pure competition and zero collaboration.

Collaboration is essential, because the world is too complex for one single expert or point of view to have the perfect solution to a problem at any given time. The multiplicity of activities occurring—in an organization, in the world—is impossible for any one person to see. You simply cannot view the whole picture. You need to be able to hear others' points of view and find where the synergy and synthesis reveal the whole picture of what's going on. Competition and collaboration are both necessary in organizations. As always, it's about finding the right ratio.

Pause. Think of a time you have seen a collaborative project go completely awry. There is a reason people joke so much about the painful nature of team projects. Why is that? What went wrong in your experience? Was there someone in the team seen as an instigator—or was there a lack of instigation to activity at all?

Consider these three ideas to help hold the tension as you move between competition and collaboration:

1. **Bring all of your attention, authentically.** If you think being online via video allows you to multitask, you are sadly mistaken. Turn off the other things that might be causing your attention to drift away. Challenge yourself to be in full attention, cultivating the opportunity to bring all of yourself authentically. You always notice when someone isn't fully present in a conversation; don't be that person. Notice how much easier creating respectful relationships becomes for you. By practicing full attention, you short-circuit past habits. This is a step toward adopting a generative mindset that perceives everyone as whole, resourceful, capable, and creative.

2. **Learn to open your listening.** Embrace the childlike state of being in wonder of the world. I know, as parents, we think, *if I hear "why" one more time, I'm going to scream*. However, the *why* is simply a child trying to find their place in the world— and, regardless of age, we all want to discover our place in

the world. Quiet your mind, and release the need to know the answer. Listen to your teammates without criticism or a desire to make them wrong. Open your mind, and listen to what they say without wanting to fix, advise, or caretake the person. When you're an open listener, you can naturally use curiosity to learn about another. Engage in conversations for learning to demonstrate respect and genuine interest, inviting others to come into the collaborative discussion. This way of championing curiosity creates a competitive edge—because your people are the only source of that. You've chosen the workforce you have on purpose because you saw skills, knowledge, ability, and character traits that you realized will help create the unique customer experience you want. Don't discount that now.

3. **Shift the conversation away from "right" versus "wrong."** Instead, notice what works and what's better. Right-versus-wrong thinking breeds the bias that there is one right answer, and anything else is the wrong answer. The world is way too dynamic for this to be true. It's way too complex and unpredictable, with new influences arising quickly. Honestly collaborate with your team members, discussing what you see in them and what they see in you. Create a relationship on the premise, "We are in this together." This approach signals deep respect for the other person. The care and the dignity that respect evokes are critical for human beings to experience a sense of belonging—the essential intrinsic motivator to nurture.

If you follow these three practices, you will utterly transform the experience of this tension. In the process, you can learn to invite others to embody a helpful ratio between competition and collaboration—a ratio that you can trust will be appropriate for any context.

HOLD THE TENSION OF APATHY AND INSPIRATION

Destructive leaders are a source of apathy. Constructive leaders—those who create a workplace climate where people want to be—are a source of inspiration. I guess you know which one you want to be. I always include this point last on my list of common leadership dilemmas because, to me, it truly highlights the end goal: creating a space where your workers can feel safe and happy. At the moment, most employees don't seem to feel this way. Remember, 98 percent of people on the job are looking for another job.[17]

When people get disappointed repeatedly, what do they do? They wallow in victimhood. That's apathy. It starts with an emotional insecurity, which then may transfer to an economic or physical insecurity, and then continues to inertia, which is a synonym for apathy. In organizational life, this is where engagement tanks. Employees don't feel recognized, don't feel they have autonomy, and don't feel that they belong. As a leader this is what you must counter.

Have you noticed how hard it is to get another person's attention today? What do you do when people, team members, or stakeholders are apathetic about what you're working on? How do you move them to inspiration?

Gallup first began reporting on employee engagement in the 1990s. Since then, they report that the highest percentage of engaged employees in the US was 36 percent in 2020. This number fell to

---

17   Jessica Dickler, "96% of Workers Are Looking for a New Job in 2023, Poll Says," CNBC, January 13, 2023, https://www.cnbc.com/2023/01/13/96percent-of-workers-are-looking-for-a-new-job-in-2023.html.

34 percent in 2022, and the downward trend has continued since.[18] Further, lack of engagement isn't insular. Research on women in the workforce published in the *Harvard Business Review* defines the "actively disengaged" as "those who have miserable work experiences and spread their unhappiness to their colleagues."[19] I hope this data catches your attention!

Leaders of leaders have a primary job: create an environment through which everybody in the workforce feels the necessary safety, aspiration, and alignment to contribute. Contribution occurs as each person commits all of who they are, even beyond what they think is possible for themselves. This creates the level of invitation within the enterprise needed to drive mission and vision fulfillment. Leaders can continuously evolve the culture in which they work to sustain organizational excellence, which translates to the customer and feeds customer loyalty.

However, tension commonly arises in the form of apathy. The quality of apathy starts internally, within a person (and is therefore invisible to the leader). In the individual's mind, it might sound like this: *I'm going to hold my energy back on certain things that I'm doing. I'm going to slow down on the things that stress me out (apathy) so that I can feel better (inspiration) doing other activities.* This thinking results in symptoms long after the internal shift begins—symptoms like missed deadlines and poor information sharing, which can, in turn, create negativity within and across teams. When apathy lingers, it becomes contagious.

---

18   Jim Harter, "U.S. Employee Engagement Drops for First Year in a Decade," Gallup, January 7, 2022, https://www.gallup.com/workplace/388481/employee-engage-ment-drops-first-year-decade.aspx.

19   Rasmus Hougaard, Jacqueline Carter, and Marissa Afton, "When Women Leaders Leave, the Losses Multiply," *Harvard Business Review*, March 8, 2022, https://hbr.org/2022/03/when-women-leaders-leave-the-losses-multiply.

Discovering what stimulates apathy drives healthier choices across an enterprise and shifts the focus of the workforce to what inspiration reveals: new possibilities for learning, development, and contribution. Your best resource is to remember that pause gives more time than it takes. Leaders who stay with a problem—even in discomfort—and embrace curiosity and wonder can see that many multiple worthy answers exist for every question. Examining problems more deeply through the lens of either of the tension qualities creates a giant playground, one the leader can explore to determine solutions to thorny issues. The presence of tension, tolerated for a little bit longer, became a way to foster freedom, turning what at first appears to be damaging (apathy) into a resource for perceiving what change to invite and, through that, to generate a more desirable state (inspiration).

 Pause. Now, be really, really honest with yourself. In the course of your career, was there ever a point where you just said to yourself, "You know what? I just don't care." Think back to the emotions that incited. It probably didn't feel great, showing up to work each day when your heart wasn't in it. Nobody enjoys apathy. An apathetic teammate? They don't enjoy feeling that way! Remember that.

Consider these three ideas to help hold the tension as you move between apathy and inspiration:

1. **Conduct a *workforce* stay interview.** When the quality of apathy is unrecognized or ignored, the cost of inaction is great—because the end result is a lack of the action required

to deliver customer outcomes. Similar to a "stay interview" with an individual, consider the following questions a way to explore a workforce "stay interview." The aim is to reveal the current tension between the qualities of apathy and inspiration in your workplace.

- What have you been ignoring?

- What is your cue to be authentic and bold and inspire a new team environment?

- What inspires you right now?

- And what would you share with your team?

- What is the structure you want in place to support and continue the evolution of your team's climate?

- What do you want to shift and produce differently in the employee experience?

The central idea offered by these questions empowers leaders to answer an overarching question: "How do I learn to tolerate the tension present and use curiosity and wonder to discover the rest of the story?"

2. **Believe what you experience beyond what you hear.** Active listening is one of those things I'm sure you've learned a lot about along the way. I want to challenge your assumptions; you don't know everything there is to know about active listening. What's important here is to realize you must *listen beyond the words.* Your sensory systems always receive clues about the experiences of other people. Unfortunately, you don't always pay attention to those clues. Experiencing another person means you're observing with your instinct and intuition. You may have a limited amount of practice

paying attention to the wide range of ways you experience another person. This is your opportunity. Suppose you give more attention to perceiving what someone *means* but doesn't say. This is a game changer in demonstrating respect, confidence, and trust in the other person's point of view.

3. **Adopt patience as your invitation to receive from others.** It's easy to shortcut your interactions in the workplace based on your assumptions. You anticipate and then listen to see if your assumption confirms what you perceive about the person and the situation. Unfortunately, this signals to the other person that you don't want to know what they think or what they might contribute, beyond what you already know. You create a partnership when you replace your assumptions with curiosity and then let yourself wonder, giving your rapt attention and astonishment to the other's perspective. When you move too quickly from assumption to action, you fail to create a partnership, generating resistance to inspiration. Spend more time and energy on observing and listening internally. Try to see what your intuition picks up—what you're sensing in the other person's point and its impact on you. Be open about what is happening and invite the other to participate. Ask, "How do we navigate this unknown territory together?"

Be thoughtful about your active listening, presence, and perception. As a leader, you want to telegraph the relevant and valuable balance between apathy and inspiration. If you follow these three practices, you will utterly transform the experience of this tension and invite others to do the same.

Inspiring Leadership Demands Deliberate Judgment

What's your job, as a leader? Maybe you'll tell me it's to inspire or motivate. Maybe you'll tell me it's to educate. I'd say it just boils down to one thing: as a leader, your job is to shape a world where people love their life's work. That's it. That is every leader's job. Learning to sit in the tensions that invariably arise in the workplace, instead of steamrolling over them (and, in the process, over people), is a critical component of creating that kind of psychologically safe space—one where people can show up authentically and express themselves fearlessly.

Creating that kind of psychological safety requires you to reexamine your own habits, preferences, assumptions, and biases. This is a pivotal step in ACAAR that occurs after you reflect on what happened and before you construct a new way forward. It's essential to exercise what I call *deliberate* judgment if you want to sustain excellence with the new path you choose to construct. Deliberate judgment is often misunderstood, as "judgment" is conflated with the negative connotations of being judgmental. In the next chapter, I'd like to set the record straight and explain exactly why I'm a champion of *deliberate* judgment—and just what I mean by that.

EXERCISE: IDENTIFY YOUR JUDGMENT AS A LEADER

The chapter 2 concluding exercise had you consider an instance that occurred in which the actions pursued did not produce a satisfactory result.

Revisit these four questions with a wider lens that considers how you show up as a leader for your team, and for your peer colleagues, as everyone pursues fulfillment of the organization's mission.

The four questions in the following diagram offer a way to surface what motivates your chosen actions so that you can begin to understand how mindset can operate quite invisibly unless you pause and ask questions that break the unconscious patterns of behavior that habit, preference, assumption, and bias activate.

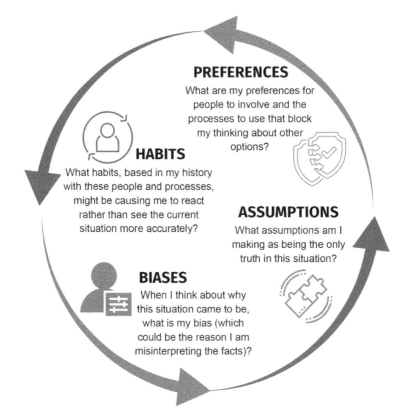

PREFERENCES
What are my preferences for people to involve and the processes to use that block my thinking about other options?

HABITS
What habits, based in my history with these people and processes, might be causing me to react rather than see the current situation more accurately?

ASSUMPTIONS
What assumptions am I making as being the only truth in this situation?

BIASES
When I think about why this situation came to be, what is my bias (which could be the reason I am misinterpreting the facts)?

Answer all four questions. Answer in any order. Start with the easiest one.

1. What are my preferences for the people to involve and the processes to use that block my thinking about other options to organize how we fulfill the mission?

2. What habits, based on my history with these people and processes, might be causing me to react rather than see the organization's current situation more accurately?

3. What assumptions am I making as being the only truth in the current environment?

4. When I think about why the organization is in the current environment it is, what is my bias (which could be the reason I am misinterpreting the facts)?

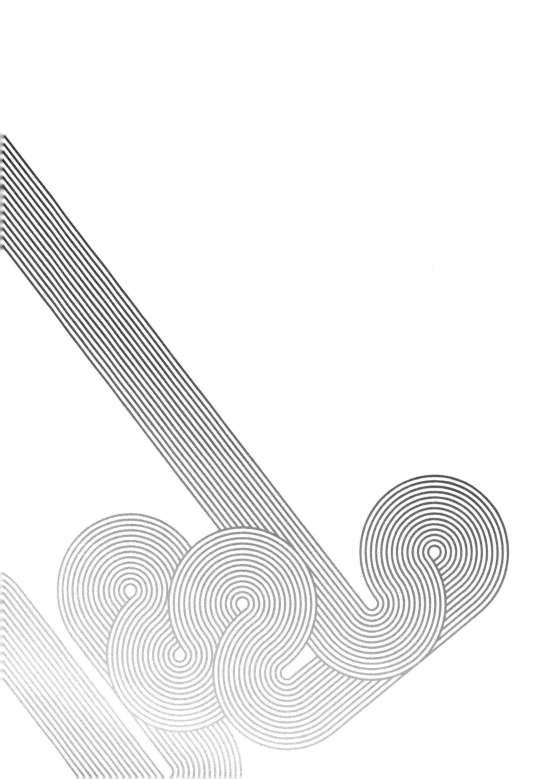

CHAPTER 6

DELIBERATE JUDGMENT

Failures are a part of life. If you don't fail, you will never learn. If you don't learn, you will never change.

—UNKNOWN

Y ou've probably been walking around in the land of judgment in the previous chapter. As you've examined novel ways of managing the seven common dilemmas of leadership and started to engage with the ACAAR model, some uncomfortable memories may have started to bubble up. And as you completed the previous end-of-chapter exercise, you may have faced unwelcome truths about your habits, preferences, assumptions, and biases.

You may have reminisced about all the moments when you felt judgmental—in the negative, destructive sense—and acted from emotionality. Maybe you shut down an employee. Maybe you said something you now regret. Maybe you failed to close the feedback loop in a constructive way. As you've widened your lens to reexamine those situations, you've probably started to ask yourself, *Did I really have the whole story? Even if I thought I had the whole story, did I trust that somebody always has a different point of view? Did I have the patience to go and find out the other point of view?*

In short, you've started to question your mindset. That's a troubling place to be. As I mentioned in the very first pages of this book, leaders tend to adopt an identity, both to achieve and to avoid feeling uncomfortable. Shaking that identity, even for the better, creates tension. However, you're now learning how to sit in that tension.

Pause. Check in with yourself. How are you feeling at this point in the book? Disheartened? Inspired? Regretful? Optimistic? Jot down your feelings now. If you're feeling low energy, take a break. Talk to a friend. Put the book down. It will still be here when you get back. After all, there's still work to do—and the best is yet to come.

Here is your opportunity to start trusting in the unknown. You're not in a bad place. It may be an unnerving place, yes. It's certainly an unfamiliar place. But it's also going to allow you to enter a more productive place—a generative state.

To get there, you've got to harness that nasty judgment you've been grappling with in the previous chapter and reframe it. You've got to make it deliberate. Deliberate judgment, the kind I want you to engage with, comes only once you recognize and look beyond your own habits, preferences, assumptions, and biases. Let's look at how to do that.

What Do I Mean by Deliberate Judgment?

Remember the definition of "judgment"? Let's refresh: judgment is "the ability to form valuable opinions and make good decisions."[20] Judgment has many negative connotations in modern society, especially Western Anglophone society. We've collapsed the definitions of "judgment" and "judgmental" and come to place a huge premium on zero judgment. However, this makes it difficult to enact curiosity, let alone wonder. It also tends to squash truth-telling—which, in some cases, can be harmful.

Consider this: when there is something disrupting a relationship or a situation, we default to a nonjudgmental state. We're conditioned to be nice, kind, and respectful and to give grace. The problem is that by staying silent in those situations, we carry the suffering and the burden of the impact of that behavior on ourselves. Our perception becomes skewed when we abandon all judgment.

Judgment is, at its very core definition, not a bad thing. There is nothing negative about considered, forming of valuable opinions and making good decisions. That's all that judgment is.

Now, add the word "deliberate" in front of it. Deliberate simply means "intentional or planned."[21] When I ask you to exercise deliberate judgment, I'm just asking you to make considered decisions consciously and intentionally and, through them, to reach sensible conclusions. The issue is that so much of our exercise of judgment is

---

20 *Cambridge Advanced Learner's Dictionary*, 4th ed. (Cambridge: Cambridge University Press, 2013), s.v. "Judgment," https://dictionary.cambridge.org/dictionary/english/judgment.

21 *Cambridge Advanced Learner's Dictionary*, 4th ed. (Cambridge: Cambridge University Press, 2013), s.v. "Deliberate," https://dictionary.cambridge.org/dictionary/english/deliberate.

not deliberate; rather, it's rooted in habits, preferences, assumptions, and biases.

This is actually why ACAAR has that extra "A" in the middle! True story: when we first developed the concept, it was ACAR. Only later did we add the "Alignment" step and ask people to consider the basis of their decisions—what habits, preferences, assumptions, and biases informed their point of view. We added that step, because we realized that if we didn't investigate what was motivating the faulty premise for a decision, we weren't getting the full story, and learning and growth would be hindered as a result.

An anecdote from the banking sector can help demonstrate what I mean. Community banking illustrates an important hallmark in American society. It was once considered vitally important to be part of a banking "family" locally, across generations, by being accessible, relevant, and personal in every interaction at every touchpoint with the customer. Continuity with that history applies to both products and the characteristic behaviors of the workforce that sustain that "family."

However, this foundational premise produces a dilemma for community bank management. How do they determine how to take advantage of their past while moving into new opportunities—like online banking? How do they exploit the old and explore the new? In what ways can the bank use components of its past as building blocks to realize its future strategic vision?

One of my clients faced just this set of challenges, with the executive management team feeling a push-and-pull struggle to stay relevant in their community while also needing to modernize to survive in a highly competitive market. The US East Coast was being flooded with new banks without the overhead of lots and lots of brick-and-mortar (literally) branch offices. How could they ever hope to keep up?

In the worst-case scenario, they might have jumped on a "quick fix" solution. Instead, they took time to pause and consider. As a group, the executive leaders examined their product lines and lines of business. They realized they were very effective at product ideation and evolution, that is, how to reinvigorate, change, and even "delete" unwanted products or services. In the past, these ideas had been spoken out loud—but forgotten when it came time to make decisions and fund implementation.

As a result, they ended up with a massive line of products and services, many of them without real benefit. The cost to operations was huge. Additionally, there was a great deal of employee confusion about what was a priority for customers. Adding to that complexity was the question of a potential bank restructure, with the idea of an initial public offering (IPO) on the table. How might an IPO influence desired changes to the customer experience?

Excellence in performance was deemed a "must-have" regardless of corporate structure. The management team identified three components needed to fulfill the value proposition for customers: quality service, trustworthy care, and community presence. The conversation also allowed them to identify failure points in their change leadership strategy that could be fixed before rolling out a new customer strategy to the workforce—such as the pitfall of delivering customer care without consideration for customer value.

These discussions led to identifying a wide variety of obstacles, all of which they could exercise deliberate judgment to resolve. Up until that point, they had never stopped to notice what was motivating the habits and biases holding those obstacles in place. It took a central obstacle—the sense of urgency regarding the bank's survivability in the face of a tough competitive climate—to inspire these discussions. Again, the management could have sought a rapid resolution instead of taking time to pause and reflect. Instead, they held the tension.

Sustaining their customer strategy became the key to successful culture change. Results produce change—not the other way around. Reconstructing the business processes, workforce communications, internal training and rewards programs, and external marketing to customers now had a common focus. Through conscious declaration, the bank's team spoke with one voice about what to prioritize in their change effort to achieve sustainability. And that they did, with great success.

> Is there a time in your career where you resorted to a rapid response in order to seek a solution? Did it turn out as you'd hoped? Alternatively, can you identify a time where you resisted the urge to act fast and acted deliberately instead? How did that turn out?

Deliberate Judgment, Deliberate Mindset

Part of the reason it's so tricky to engage in deliberate judgment is that your innate judgment—the one informed by habits, preferences, assumptions, and biases—is part of your mindset. If you're like most people, you probably spend little to no time thinking about your mindset during your daily life. Usually, life gives you feedback about your mindset when you react to a situation or event in an unhealthy manner. Sometimes, we catch that ourselves. However, usually, it's external feedback that throws it in our faces.

I often see this in my clients in the form of physical breakdown. One coaching partner of mine, I'll call her Janelle, was under great stress professionally for an extended period. Unfortunately, she developed chronic pain, which has been shown to be linked to stress.[22] It wasn't until her body gave her this painful feedback and raised the red flag that she realized just how damaging the constant stress she was under really was. Her mindset was so attuned to professional success that she valued it even above personal well-being. It took a massive mindset shift to recalibrate.

Health examples like this one are, unfortunately, prevalent in the high-performing world. Mental health is even more disregarded in some cases. A friend of mine recently got a fitness tracker. She was telling me about it, and I noticed that she fixated only on the physical components: heart rate, blood pressure, oxygen saturation, and so on. However, this device also has a mental health side to it. It offers free meditations, for instance, and lets you log your moods so that you can start to identify patterns of stressors in your life.

We had a conversation about it, and she admitted, "I disregard the mental health part because I don't want to make time for it." She would spend one hour at the gym, but she wouldn't spend five minutes on a stress-reducing meditation. That alone spoke to her mindset—attentiveness to physical health took precedent, while mental health fell by the wayside (despite the known interplay between physical and mental well-being).

---

22   Chadi G. Abdallah and Paul Geha, "Chronic Pain and Chronic Stress: Two Sides of the Same Coin?" *Chronic Stress (Thousand Oaks)* 1 (2017), https://doi.org/10.1177/24705470177047.

That blew my mind, especially because she herself admitted that she struggles with stress and that it impacts her personal relationships. She told me, "I can't see my partner right after the workday, because I'll snap at them about something stupid. I need at least an hour or two—which is unfortunate, because we both work a lot and that's precious time we don't have together." And I said, "Well, what if you try one of those meditations from your fitness tracker to come down after work? Maybe that one or two hours could be ten or twenty minutes, so you get more of that quality time you want." For her, it was an illuminating moment about her own mindset and how a shift toward placing greater value on mental well-being might benefit her.

Mindset has a huge impact on our lives. It influences how we show up for ourselves and in our interpersonal relationships—as seen in the example. In the workplace, leaders must consider the many different mindsets of their employees and how those play into workplace relationships and interactions. However, first, leaders must take a long hard look at their own mindset.

Your mindset is formed by a collection of your thoughts and beliefs. Those thoughts and beliefs shape your habits and actions. They influence how you think, what you feel, and what you choose to do. Your mindset helps you make sense of the world, how you show up in the world, and the impact you have on others. It is how you react to success, setbacks, and everything in between. Your most reliable change strategy is your mindset.

> **Your most reliable change strategy is your mindset.**

However, too often we cling to outdated mindsets. Mindset shift is an underdeveloped capacity in everyone. Remember that timeline exercise in chapter 3? That involved taking an inventory of pivotal moments in your life—moments that helped shape your worldview— and considering how those past moments shape your current interactions and reactions—your mindset! Notice what that exercise revealed that operates on autopilot, which means you don't likely share it with anyone, unless they are curious enough to ask.

The point of the exercise was to get you to ask yourself, *Is that still relevant now?* That's a question you've got to ask yourself again and again as you walk through life. If you want to change the world, you must strengthen your capacity to recognize and evolve your own mindset and encourage everyone around you to do so as well. Just as the natural world is in constant evolution, you are too. Creating a natural rhythm of personal change also allows you to bring others current with your mindset and invite them to share theirs with you.

American psychologist Dr. Carol S. Dweck is known for her work about the psychological traits of a person's mindset. She's a pioneering researcher in the field of motivation and why people succeed or don't. Her work coined the terms "fixed mindset" and "growth mindset." Each term describes the underlying beliefs people have about learning and intelligence—beliefs that can help explain why some people are successful and others are not.

In a fixed mindset, people believe their basic qualities, such as their intelligence or talent, are simply fixed traits. They spend their time documenting their intelligence or talent instead of developing them. They also believe that talent alone creates success, without effort. Inherent in this mindset is a perspective looking at the rearview mirror rather than the front windshield. As time passes and the surrounding ecosystem evolves, this mindset loses relevance quickly.

By contrast, in a growth mindset, people believe that their most basic abilities can be developed through dedication and hard work— brains and talent are just the starting point. This view creates a love of learning and a resilience that is essential for great accomplishment. Having a growth mindset creates a thirst for learning, nurtures a motivation to discover new things, and establishes a desire to work through challenges and grow as a person. When people with a growth mindset try and fail, they tend not to view it as a failure or disappointment. Instead, it is a learning experience that can lead to growth and change.

QUICK ACTIVITY: CHALLENGE YOUR MINDSET

When is the last time you actively considered your mindset? Do you give it any thought now? Have you ever? To develop a growth mindset for navigating the tensions of presence, let's return to our three micro-skills from chapter 4:

1. See that a situation is worthy of pausing.

2. Notice all that's occurring to recognize unconscious choices and choose consciously.

3. Stay with the question(s) that reveal motivation and be deliberate moving forward.

To pay attention to your thoughts, actions, and behaviors, you must engage in a deliberate process. Use the following table to start a daily five-minute practice of writing down what you notice. Do this for the situations that are producing the greatest tension for you—where the payout for this activity will make the greatest impact in your daily experience. The act of writing down what you notice has two positive outcomes: you evoke conscious awareness inside of you, and you stimulate curiosity essential to learning about your internal motivation. This also creates accountability to ensure you are on the path for developing and fostering a growth mindset.

I like this simple spreadsheet myself, because I don't want to expend extra effort, but I do want to see my results continuously so that I can acknowledge progress and course correct as needed. The spreadsheet does the proverbial math for me, and I can see my accountability at a glance. Four weeks is typically enough time to build a new habit, so that's what's included here. However, you can always go longer as your learning insights influence how you produce new, more favorable results.

Month/Year: _____

Habit Goals: *Complete all three skills five out of seven days of the week*

	Weekly Target	Week 1							Weekly Total	Week 2							Weekly Total
EMPOWERING HABIT		M	T	W	T	F	S	S		M	T	W	T	F	S	S	
See a situation worthy of pause																	
Notice thoughts, actions, and behaviors																	
Ask questions that reveal my motivation																	

	Weekly Target	Week 3							Weekly Total	Week 4							Weekly Total
EMPOWERING HABIT		M	T	W	T	F	S	S		M	T	W	T	F	S	S	
See a situation worthy of pause																	
Notice thoughts, actions, and behaviors																	
Ask questions that reveal my motivation																	

Consider these questions to start your journey. Your answers can help you create a positive structure to form new habits:

- Where do you focus your attention during the day?

  □ What does your daily routine look like?

  □ As a counterpoint, what can you learn from adopting new routines?

- Where does your motivation and inspiration come from?

  □ What are your goals?

  □ What values help you accomplish them?

  □ As a counterpoint, what daily decisions do you make from habit and preference—and how might more intentional, values-aligned decisions deliver more satisfying and useful outcomes?

- Who do you surround yourself with?

  □ Are they people who look and act like you?

- As a counterpoint, what can you learn by diversifying who you surround yourself with?

- What's possible when you open your mind and heart to new perspectives?

Exploring these questions can help you adopt practices that sustain your connection to a mindset for development, growth, and positive change. Strengthen your sovereign expression by integrating self, family, community, workplace, society, and the planet into your rubric for leading well.

The Impact of Leadership Mindset on the Workplace

When your environment becomes highly complex, ambiguous, and volatile, becoming aware of and intentional with your mindset before you interact or make decisions produces better outcomes. Conversely, when you allow the timeline and external demands to override your natural rhythm to be thoughtful, inclusive, and balanced, the shortcut of reacting without thoughtfulness or intention can create negative consequences for you and those around you.

In the previous chapter, I have shared what I consider the leader's job: to shape a world where people love their life's work. At the moment, many leaders appear to be failing on that point. Consider some of the statistics from Gallup's *2023 State of the Global Workplace* report: only 23 percent of employees are "thriving" at work, 18 percent are loud quitting, and 59 percent are quiet quitting.[23] How did we get here?

---

23   "State of the Global Workplace: 2023 Report," Gallup, 2023, https://www.gallup.com/workplace/349484/state-of-the-global-workplace.aspx.

From my perspective, part of the problem is that leaders aren't living in a state of Generative Wholeness™. By being generative, we collectively produce the conditions by which each person enthusiastically accepts responsibility to live in wholeness. I think we're seeing a craving for "wholeness" in what Gartner refers to as a desire for "The Human Deal." Employees are seeking humanity at work in the form of five things: deeper connections, radical flexibility, personal growth, holistic well-being, and shared purpose.

> **By being generative, we collectively produce the conditions by which each person enthusiastically accepts responsibility to live in wholeness.**

Companies aren't immune to this kind of data. Some are trying to pivot, with varying degrees of success. For example, one trend I'm seeing now in the companies I work with is a desire for more social connection within the company. It's recognized that social connection fosters a more engaged work environment. Surveys have shown people who have a work pal are more likely to stay with a company and be satisfied at work, for instance.[24]

Now, companies *do* hear the ask. But delivering on that ask proves problematic—in part, due to mindset hurdles. A recent meeting I had with a leadership team spoke to this. They told me, "Yes, our team members want more social time. Yes, we as a leadership team want more social time with each other. But we don't have the time." They had very aggressive sales targets and could not fathom taking time away from those performance goals for socializing. So, they didn't. Minutes equaled money, in their minds.

---

24   Jon Clifton, "The Power of Work Friends," *Harvard Business Review*, October 7, 2022, https://hbr.org/2022/10/the-power-of-work-friends.

This was creating a vicious cycle. They weren't retaining staff. In fact, when I met them, they were woefully understaffed—in part because they were hemorrhaging talent. The company culture was not convincing people to stick around. Being understaffed then put more pressure on the remaining employees to meet their performance goals. The time crunch intensified. The likelihood of making time for socializing became even less.

The truth was that there was *always* going to be some reason why there wouldn't be time for socializing. Time became the convenient bogeyman in this case. The problem is that when people identify an external bogeyman, they lose control. They're no longer operating from a place of sovereignty or self-accountability. It's a self-created prison.

At this point, one of two things could have happened: the leadership team could have continued on the same path, with the employees suffering for want of socializing—or the leadership team could exercise deliberate judgment and question their mindset to break out of that prison they'd created. Luckily, they chose the latter.

In this case, deliberate judgment required the leadership team to examine their own habits, preferences, assumptions, and biases. Their habit was to focus only on outcomes—concrete performance goals like sales figures (a common habit among leadership). This led to a narrow view that neglected other aspects of what helps a company thrive—like an engaged workforce. It was only once they recognized their bias toward quantitative results and connected these dots that the leadership team was able to take a different action—namely, carving out time for socializing. Mind you, not just any socializing but rather deliberate socializing. The kind that built trusting relationships and unleashed discretionary energy from team members who felt more respected by their leaders and were given greater autonomy to act.

In some ways, being deliberate becomes a process of connecting the dots across decisions. Failure to connect the dots for the workforce becomes the greatest source of resistance to change. This ultimately limits the risk-taking needed to remain competitive and responsive to changes in both the marketplace and customer needs.

Connecting dots across decisions is another seemingly simple concept that companies consistently avoid. Usually, they identify individual reasons in the rearview mirror without really seeking links. They'll say, "Last time we did end up with a big reduction in force because we miscalculated the revenue forecast," or "We trusted the vendor's guidance about training requirements. That's why we ended up delivering the new technology one year late and losing customer loyalty from overpromising our service improvements."

Such examples—and the ones before it—highlight the challenge of multiplicity. When there are many factors at play, which there inevitably are in today's complex world, there's a greater risk of mental blinders and emotional barriers. You can't expect the workforce to see clearly. Building awareness requires deliberate judgment, followed by desire, and, finally, knowledge. Only then can you realize new actions that produce new results.

In these examples, the leadership, with a little help from their coach, began to see that their attachment to past experiences and perceived failures was creating an obstacle. They had to pause and notice how the current moment was different. They also had to acknowledge that they were different—wiser, in fact—and that they had a choice to construct a better outcome with that hard-won wisdom. Discussion helped the teams question their own biases and widen their lens to exercise deliberate judgment, based on the reality of the *current* situation and team members involved. This allowed for the mindset shift that produced a shift in action—to create space and time for more social connection in the workplace as a deliberate act to drive higher performance that teams would enthusiastically sustain.

 Looking back on your career, was there a time when you neglected to connect the dots? You probably played "connect the dots" as a kid, maybe in some old coloring book. The next time you are facing a decision-making process informed by tension, pull out your metaphorical crayon and get ready to connect the dots.

Notice Judgment to Deepen Learning and Step into Authenticity

Judge deliberately. Choose your mindset deliberately. Your mindset and the ability to swiftly shift your mindset become your biggest asset. It determines whether you are committed to achieving your goals when things get tough. Life ebbs and flows, and a sovereign mindset gives you the ability to adapt. It will also allow you to deepen your learning.

Remember, a growth mindset doesn't get set back by mistakes. A sovereign mindset accepts responsibility for an inner authority to choose to seize on mistakes as opportunities for development. Your deliberate judgment can deepen awareness and provide moments of insight that will put you in a generative zone.

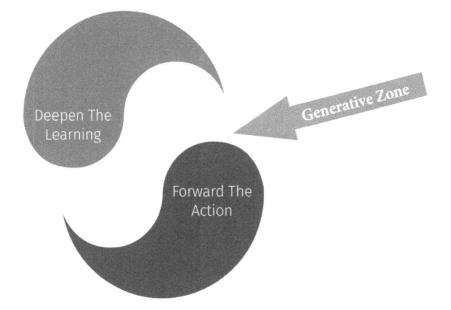

You began this chapter questioning your habits, preferences, assumptions, and biases. This is the first step in exercising deliberate judgment—and, in turn, adapting your mindset. This will make it easier to come up with new solutions when thorny problems arise, like those dilemmas outlined in the previous chapter. Consider your mindset as a beautiful piece of marble that you can visualize a magnificent statue out of. You are the sculptor, chipping away the stone that is unnecessary and manifesting the beauty that will radiate from the inside out.

Being attentive to your mindset and learning how to evolve it will also help you achieve more of those moments of bliss discussed in the first chapter. That bliss is found in your authentic self, of which your mindset is a part. It's never too late to get back to that self—not necessarily easy but not too late, ever.

I have a deep admiration for people who tune back into their authentic selves later in life, at a time when thinking tends to become more calcified and change more challenging. Consider individuals who have illustrious careers in deeply analytical roles and then retire to take up the arts. James Comey left the Federal Bureau of Investigation (FBI) to become a fiction novelist, for instance. One of my clients, a software guy with a highly technical mind, happens to be a music buff. He's a coach himself, and one thing he loves to do is make playlists for his clients. He's attuned to his authentic self and brings it to his interactions. He doesn't leave that part of him out in his professional relationships because it's important to him. That kind of wholeness sustains an authentic, fulfilling life.

Deliberate judgment and authentic self are closely intertwined. Judgment is the extrinsic—how you relate to the situation and deliberately question your interpretations of it. To be good at that process of deliberate judgment, you need to know your authentic self. At the same time, you can't remain attuned to your authentic self without regularly exercising deliberate judgment. It's a very reciprocal relationship, one we'll examine more closely in the next chapter.

> I have a deep admiration for people who tune back into their authentic selves later in life, at a time when thinking tends to become more calcified and change more challenging.

EXERCISE: CONSTRUCT A NEW APPROACH TO SOLUTIONS

The chapter 2 concluding exercise had you consider an instance that occurred in which the actions pursued did not produce a satisfactory result.

In the chapter 5 exercise, you were asked to answer four questions to illuminate what motivated those chosen actions—a first step to recognizing how mindset can operate invisibly.

This final step offers a way to construct a new approach to solutions, a means of making choices about actions based on a more holistic appreciation for the influences producing the results.

Through the lens of your new awareness, use this step-by-step method to choose the beliefs or principles that you now understand as the most important drivers—those drivers that fully align with decision-making criteria for your teams as they pursue new choices and produce new, better results.

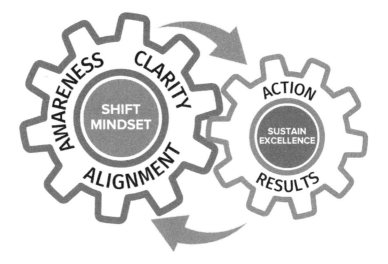

1. Awareness: Remember the beginning of the process. Now, notice what data, information, experience, or others' perspective are valuable and relevant to include for a new, more empowering choice.

2. Clarity: Notice the internal motivation or stimulus desired to make new, more empowered choices. This is often a belief.

3. Alignment: Consider what new basis supports choosing those new, empowering actions. This is often a value or principle.

4. Action: Identify the actions that produced the new desirable result.

5. Result: Describe what the new satisfactory result is.

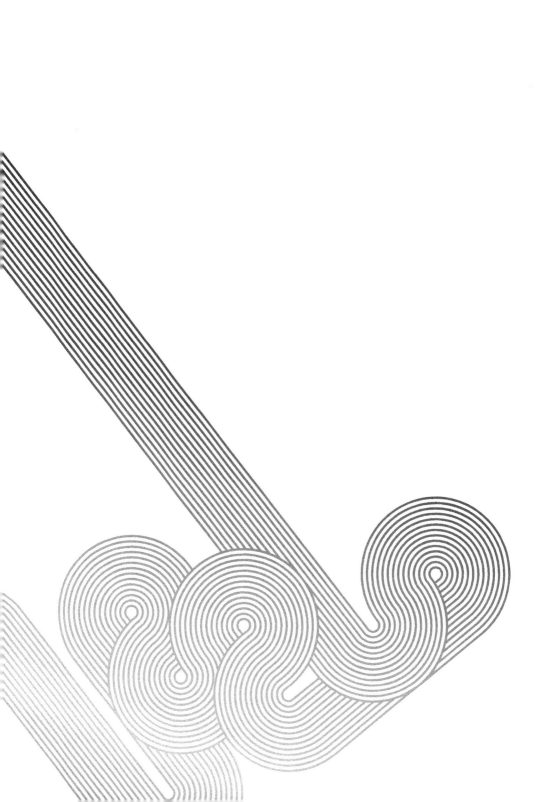

CHAPTER 7

AUTHENTIC SELF

Leaders are problem solvers by talent and
temperament, and by choice.
—HARLAN CLEVELAND, AMERICAN DIPLOMAT

D iscovering one's authentic self is a very vulnerable act. We've constructed most of our adult life, creating boundaries to keep our authentic self safe from the judgment of the world. In the very first pages of this book, I mentioned that leaders often adopt an expected identity, both to achieve and to avoid discomfort. The problem is that this often denies the authentic self.

The journey to reclaim the authentic self is often quite tender. You have layers of protection that you've set down for yourself. You adopted them at a time when you weren't quite ready to navigate the world from a place of authenticity. Perhaps you had an experience that told you authenticity wasn't a safe space to operate from. Perhaps you simply found it easier to operate from a performative identity than your true one. Perhaps someone, in so many words, told you that your authentic self was not welcome.

There are certain fears that seem to limit the authentic self, fears that many people can identify with: fear of not being important, fear of other people's opinions, fear of living up to being successful, and fear of missing out. Perhaps one of those resonates with you. These are very common fears that all humans share. Whatever your reasons, the odds are good that you have not been embracing your authentic self. Are you ready to change that?

I hope so—because the benefits of what lies on the other side, when you are prepared to operate from authenticity, are magnificent. When you are no longer at the mercy of others' opinions, you can live a life that allows you to pursue those things that truly make your heart sing—the things that give you that elusive bliss we talked about in the first chapter.

Take something as simple as a youthful passion—something you may have dropped along the way of life. Maybe it seemed "childish" or "uncool" at some point, or perhaps you didn't have time for it. The year 2023 has seen a social media trend of people rediscovering and sharing their long-lost hobbies as they enter their late thirties, forties, and beyond. Often, these are things that the individual disavowed as they "grew up," because these activities didn't support their vision of a "grownup:" Pokémon GO, geocaching, kickball, and so on.

This wave of people rediscovering their youthful passions and finding joy in them is one small example of the personal benefits that come with reclaiming authenticity. These individuals may have once been held back by worries of others' perceptions of them. No more. Perhaps it was a knee-jerk reaction to the COVID-19 pandemic, a reminder to all of us that time is precious, and we must use it wisely—

and what better way than in the pursuit of simple bliss? That is what reclaiming your authenticity can give you: simple bliss.

 Can you remember a time when you felt the need to hide your authentic self? How did it feel? Alternatively, can you remember a time when someone encouraged you to tap into your authenticity? How did that feel?

Authentic Self: The Gift You Give Yourself—and Then to Others

There are also professional benefits to rediscovering that authenticity—although sometimes we need some hand-holding to find it. And that is where great leadership can make a difference. A friend of mind, I'll call her Alison, still fondly remembers a boss she had in her mid-twenties who helped her toward her authentic self. She was stuck in a dead-end editorial role in the travel and tourism sector, writing and revising website content for a hotel booking platform. She was bored and disengaged.

Her boss, recognizing her apathy, asked her if she'd be interested in a new project—creating an internal digital newsletter to help share updates between the various branch offices. According to the boss, the sole aim was to align the disparate offices more cohesively. Alison agreed, and she greatly enjoyed the project. After that first newsletter went out, she felt a sense of accomplishment she hadn't felt for years. Her boss then revealed why he'd offered her this project (surprise,

surprise, it wasn't *just* for the company's gain), telling her, "You are the type of person who needs to create something tangible in your work. You need to see or hold something at the end of the day or the month or the year and be able to say, 'I made this.'"

She was floored—because he was spot-on. Her leader had recognized this trait in her, without her ever fully realizing and articulating it for herself. Her leader had operated much in the way a good coach does, by identifying part of her authentic self and helping her unwrap it. Alison understood that one of her values was creativity and went on to enjoy a fulfilling career that centered around exactly that premise—creating.

 Can you remember an instance where someone in your life revealed a fact about you TO you? It's like they shone a light on you. Maybe it felt like a warm glow of sunlight, as you realized something lovely about yourself. Maybe it felt like a harsh interrogation light, as you realized something not so lovely about yourself. Remember that moment now. Were you astonished? Did it make you curious to explore that part of yourself? If you never did, are you ready to now?

That is why I always say good leaders and good coaches have much in common: they essentially help people get in touch with their own authentic selves. That begins with recognizing your own authentic self, something that must be done from the inside out, not the other way around. Leaders who live authentically implicitly invite others to do the same. This creates a safe space where there is no need for critical judgment or comparison but a celebration of diverse opinions and people—a welcoming of the common humanity that bonds us all.

There is a personal peace that comes from reclaiming the authentic self that makes it worth suffering the tenderness required for that reclaiming process. This can be one of the benefits of working with a coach, someone trained to help others identify and unpack their authenticity from the layers of protective paper and ribbon it's wrapped in. However, you don't *have* to work with a coach to unwrap this gift. There are steps you can take and self-guided activities you can do—some of them in this book—to realize it yourself.

Whatever path you take, reclaiming your authenticity will take some effort, but it *is* worth it. I genuinely believe that reclaiming the authentic self is one of the greatest gifts you can give yourself. And once you've done that, you can share that gift with others—a true testament to great leadership.

QUICK ACTIVITY: REMEMBER A SPARK OF YOUR AUTHENTIC SELF

Think of an activity you used to do that you enjoyed. Maybe it was something as simple as reading. Maybe it was creating art or chatting with an old friend or digging around in your garden or playing golf or going scuba diving.

Why did you let it fall by the wayside?

Maybe it was time or shifting priorities. Challenge yourself now—give that activity another shot. Make the time.

See if it still brings you some joy. If it does, why not make more time for it in your life?

Authentic Self: From the Inside Out

Living inside out, aware and awake, is the beginning of restoring a lifepath rooted in authenticity. This occurs when you invite enlivening wonder in place of doubt, choice in place of stuck-ness, and courage to engage others in place of isolating incivility. Claiming a true self is the first step; then, you need to live inside out, allowing yourself to break calcified thinking and to transform, evolve, and regenerate relationships with resilience.

The problem is that most people don't start on the *inside*. They start by looking at the *outside*, at the symptoms, failing to recognize the impact of living from the inside out. When dissatisfaction arises, most people start by looking at a very basic barometer everyone can understand, quality of life.

Quality of life is something we are obsessed with. There are endless surveys and studies on how to improve it and identifying the things that detract from it. There are entire quality-of-life city rankings that list cities according to the "good" or "bad" quality of life they offer, considering factors like safety, cleanliness, and access to public transportation. *U.S. News & World Report*, *The Economist*, and the Organisation for Economic Co-operation and Development (OECD) all have their own rankings, each with their own criteria and results. The sheer diversity of opinions on what impacts "quality of life" and how to define it should already be a red flag that we're going about this the wrong way.

> **The sheer diversity of opinions on what impacts "quality of life" and how to define it should already be a red flag that we're going about this the wrong way.**

I'm convinced that a person can have a wonderful quality of life even if their hometown is at the bottom of one of these lists—and that a person who lives in a city at the top of one of these lists can have an absolutely miserable quality of life. Because the secret we so often neglect is that quality of life starts on the inside. External factors can only take us so far.

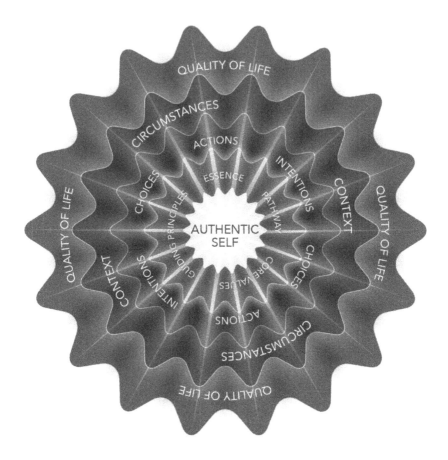

Unfortunately, most of us spend our lives looking outside of ourselves to try to improve our quality of life. We might change jobs, cities, or partners—or buy a new car, wardrobe, or house. There's a whole series of persona- and image-oriented things that we may attempt to change. Often, we are changing them based on other people; we see others as having a high quality of life and aspire to pursue that. But these kinds of changes don't work. As a result, at some point, we wake up and say, "This isn't working for me."

Think back to Alison's situation. She was at the end of her rope at her job and ready to quit. Would she have been happier if she had changed her context and shifted to a similar role at another company? Probably not. Yet she was convinced that a new employer might change the game and improve her quality of life. Instead, her quality of life changed when she became more aligned with her authentic self and was able to live that self through her daily work.

Trying to shift from the outside-in does not work. Instead, you've got to come home to your authentic self, the center ring in the diagram. The elements of the authentic self are made up of your core values, guiding principles, pathway practices, and essence—essence being your true self, stripped of the convenience of personality. The sticky thing is that these essential traits are like breathing for us, so we're not very good at identifying them. We often learn about our essence from the way people reflect back to us—the experience they have when they're listening to us, observing us, and interacting with us.

Again, consider Alison's journey. She had this innate value, creativity, that she hadn't even recognized in herself. It took a good leader to identify that value and guide her to it, not by telling her but by showing her. By giving her a project that allowed her to exercise her creativity, he opened her eyes to a sliver of her own authentic self.

That's how the journey starts. It starts with that flicker of recognition, "Oh, yeah, that's true about me. Right, I'd forgotten that about myself." Reclaiming the authentic self often means *remembering*, rediscovering the essential qualities of ourselves. It requires intense reflection to revisit the components that make up our authentic self, notably our:

- *Essence:* Essence is your true self, stripped of the convenience of personality. When core values, guiding principles, and pathway align, the essence can be realized. My core values, guiding principles, and pathway align in a way that allows me to stick to deadlines and live life on time—not rushed, harried, or frenzied, all characteristics that are out of line with my true self.

- *Pathway:* Pathway is about practices. It's basically asking yourself, *What are the practices I choose in my life?* Not for somebody else. For yourself. What practices will keep you connected to those essential traits of yourself once you've reclaimed them? You'll continually be presented with something new and unfamiliar in life, which can challenge your essential self. Your practices are how you remain rooted. So, I remain rooted in my core value of punctuality by planning an agenda every day. First thing in the morning, I write my to-do list, check my deadlines, and ensure I'm on track to meet them.

- *Core values:* Many people do a values clarification exercise at some point in their life. However, core values can shift with time and are something that must be revisited, again and again. For example, if your core values were shaped in college, this was a time when you were still in the cocoon of your parents' value system. You had not yet actually figured out, from inside of yourself, what you stood for. Values can also shift in terms of priority over time. When I was younger, punctuality was not always my top priority. Now, it's become more important to me.

- *Guiding principles:* If values are the *what*, guiding principles are the *how*. Guiding principles are guiding the experience of your life—whether it flows easily or not. One example of a guiding principle for myself is "early is easy." I don't want to stress about deadlines, so I leave sufficient time to get my work done. This guiding principle is informed by one of my core values, punctuality.

When you reclaim your authentic self through your essence, you are better able to counter both inner and outer critics. You are then able to set intentions, the inspired experience you desire to feel and sense. Your intention then informs your choices and actions.

That is when you can start to change the circumstances of your life in a meaningful way. *That* is when you can improve your quality of life in a way that's impactful, because it's serving your desires, not other peoples'. It all starts on the inside.

Again, the problem is that most people notice the symptoms first, like a dissatisfaction with their context or circumstances. They'll try to change those external circumstances, to no avail, because they continue to neglect the interior. That's when they hit the brick wall of "this isn't working."

When is the last time you felt "stuck"? Can you remember how you tried to fix it? Maybe you switched jobs or moved cities or ended your relationship with your partner. Did the external fix help? Why or why not?

Those moments of "this isn't working"—such as when you find yourself wanting to quit your job or move cities or whatever the case may be—are moments to pause and reflect. Too often, we barrel past these instances. But if we pause and take that moment to examine our lives and ourselves—for instance, by using the lifeline reflection exercise at the end of chapter 3 —we might get closer to discovering what's holding us back.

The lifeline exercise is basically helping to answer the question, *Who have I become?* The aim is to help you get current with who you are now and loosen your grip on an outdated idea of who you were. This gives you an opportunity to accept responsibility for your inner authority and how you relate to your life, and to make choices differently. It's a step toward sovereignty.

Generative Wholeness™ Is How You Live and Lead from the Authentic Self

In the second chapter, we have looked at how Generative Wholeness™ restores access to personal essence. Again, I see being generative as a double helix. One strand builds our generative capacities: to originate new thinking; create something tangible from that imagination; experiment to learn what is most valuable; and produce outcomes for ourselves and others that contribute to success, well-being, and a thriving life. In turn, a second strand radiates from the inside out, honoring the unique soul of each person—also known as their essence, their authentic self.

Living in the state of being that is Generative Wholeness™ allows you to choose change that sustains connection to effortless vitality, your essential traits that make you, you. This requires reflection—a practice I've reiterated again and again in this book. I hope you aren't tired of it yet, because it's going to be something you'll need for a lifetime. That act of reflection is such an important skill as a human being, and it's one of the most critical capacities if a leader is to sustain excellence and remain responsive to a dramatically changing environment, year after year after year.

Reflection requires pause. You must take the time for self-reflection if you are going to reclaim your authentic self and be fully present in your life. At the same time, as a leader, you must be able to artfully pause to stimulate another person's full presence in *their* life. Remember, once you unwrap that gift of being present for yourself, you can also give that gift to others. But how?

The International Coaching Federation has established a set of skills for a core competency titled "Maintains Presence." Anyone can use these behaviors in dialogue with another person to help fulfill a mutual goal or shared purpose. In the process, the leader can also invite that person to become closer to their own authentic self. This requires embodying, demonstrating, and radiating your authentic presence. An example can demonstrate what I mean by that.

HOW TO MAINTAIN AUTHENTIC PRESENCE WITH OTHERS: CONTINUAL REFLECTION

Authentic presence requires being completely joined with the other person in dialogue. You are connected to the *whole* of that person—who they are, what they want, how they learn and create, and what they must learn still. You demonstrate a complete curiosity, undiluted by a need to perform. If you are overly focused on performance to demonstrate your expertise, your attention becomes conditional, evaluating what the other person expects moment by moment.

Unconditional attention shifts the focus toward perceiving with the whole self to reflect full acceptance and celebration of the other person's expression. You are essentially in a partnership with the other person, willing to let them teach you; you are unafraid to be their student. Great coaches and great leaders alike tune into the *whole* of the person to learn from them.

When I began working with Gwendolyn, my job was to learn what was causing her undue friction at work. In my very first video meeting with her, I experienced an exuberant energy in the delivery of her words that did not match up with the emotional influence her narrative had on me. As I learned about her history and leadership experience, and her aspirations for engaging in a coaching partnership, the reason for the incongruence became clearer.

Gwendolyn was born into a loving family in South Carolina, with four brothers and two sisters. A woman, she was now working in a senior team of all male engineers. She had graduated at the top of her engineering class and earned her MBA. Following graduation, she was aggressively recruited to become a team member. She was well regarded in her field, as evidenced by published articles, invitations to speak at conferences, and various quality and achievement awards.

However, Gwendolyn described feeling conflicted—feeling appreciated and dismissed at the same time. When she began to describe her interactions with colleagues and the impact those were having on her sense of belonging, her habit for approaching relationships from the outside-in was revealed to me.

Perhaps you know an engineering leader in your professional circle. If so, you know that the profession places a big value on competition, quality, and recognition. Conversations among colleagues commonly require point-and-counterpoint dialogue, which generates a fair amount of creative abrasion. Taking anything personally produces a distraction and disrupts the desired co-creative flow. Sometimes the drive for excellence overrides empathy, the sensitivity, and awareness for how another person receives a communication. Failure to perceive it gets in the way of building cohesion and synergy.

In Gwendolyn's case, she experienced an escalating need to keep proving her ideas as worthy of attention and respected consideration.

In her mind, moments of misunderstandings became judgments—which contributed to an assumptive belief that her colleagues were excluding her. It wasn't just her ideas and contributions they were excluding but *her*, the person—at least, that's how she perceived it, at first.

Gwendolyn's situation shows the importance of noticing the assumptions and biases that influence how you are showing up and interacting with another person in discussion. This is where you start to let that curiosity that we've talked about bubble up. Wholeness is the resource for curiosity offered without condition, authentically, as a genuine invitation to learn about another's perspective and ideas. Together, you can then discover something new, original, and valuable to pursue.

Unfortunately, Gwendolyn's assumptive belief quickly became a confirmation bias. Enough time operating from this belief infected her listening; every conversation was received through the lens of the bias, which heard and confirmed her worst fears of exclusion. A breaking point came when she lost her temper and spoke negatively to a colleague, with an energy that was disproportionate to the situation. Feeling embarrassed and ashamed of her outburst, Gwendolyn went to her human resources partner and asked if she could work with a coach. Luckily, her curiosity opened the door to vulnerability—a vulnerability she was willing to explore.

Being open to your vulnerability in uncomfortable moments is a first step to pursuing change and dissolving calcified thinking. Then, by asking yourself open questions, you can begin to restore access to an inner resourcefulness, one that reminds you that you are more as a person than any one situation or context that temporarily feels bad. Such open questions should avoid performance-focused language about things like achievement, accomplishment, and goals. This interferes with unconditional acceptance, the key to allowing curiosity to bubble up—and a critical factor in allowing vulnerability.

Gwendolyn's first open question was, "What caused me to react so strongly to my colleague, the one person who seems to be my friend and ally on the team?" Keep in mind that open questions always have more than one right answer. By design, they invite internal reflection to awaken self-knowledge and insight about motivations that operate unconsciously as habits and preferences.

As we explored together, Gwendolyn claimed competition as a personal and professional value. She recognized that this value guided her decision-making about her education, choice of schools, how she prioritized her time, and which projects she elected to pursue. Focusing on the value of competition left little room for *not knowing*—being curious to learn about and from others—or experiencing wonder, that rapt attention and astonishment permitted when something new emerges.

As we talked, Gwendolyn began to feel embarrassed again—only this time it was because she realized how her narrow lens, focused almost exclusively on competition, created a barrier in her relationships with colleagues. She wasn't seeing them or respecting them despite feeling like *they* were not seeing or respecting *her*. As she broke free of the grip of that assumptive belief, she could widen her lens to view the situation more broadly. In this moment, Gwendolyn became aware of her inner witness.

The inner witness is the part of you that notices what is occurring and the impact it is having on you *as it is happening*, without losing presence with the other person in the dialogue. When you are attentive from wholeness, you may notice judgment and choose artful pause—which can be as slight as taking a breath—to welcome curiosity that accepts everything and builds on it with attentive wonder opposite the other. It is through your attention to other people, not your input, that you will generate curiosity-based questions and be able to invite them to share learning, thinking, and insight. This is how to create a partnership in conversation that is beneficial for both sides, without compromising your own essential strengths and authenticity.

The next step of Gwendolyn's internal reflection process involved exploring the last dozen interactions she had with different colleagues. She considered her habits and preferences first, making an inventory of how she constructed her understanding of each person and the influence that had on her choices for interacting with them. An entirely new set of assumptions came into view, as she began to notice how her own biases led her to take shortcuts in her conversations—shortcuts that then resulted in her being ignored or dismissed.

Gwendolyn began to recognize that she was part, cause, and agent of the experience she did not want to have. Far from disheartening, that realization was great news—because it meant that she could change the situation, by changing how she showed up and interacted. Gwendolyn's internal learning explained the past—and revealed that she had the inner authority to change the present and the future. However, that realization didn't come to Gwendolyn immediately. It took her time to get there.

It's important to have patience with this reflection work and resist moving to a solution too quickly. It's tempting to move quickly in order to relieve the discomfort that arises when you discover that *your* choices and actions created the breakdown. Resist the temptation, or you're in danger of missing out on a valuable solution.

In Gwendolyn's case, the next step involved constructing a new desired future that transcended her existing habits, preferences, assumptions, and biases, thereby making way for new learning. That new learning was to come through fresh dialogue with her colleagues. And that dialogue had to invite a different basis for their relationships.

Showing great courage and vulnerability, Gwendolyn began that journey with the person she lost her temper with—her friend and ally. They accepted her apology and partnered with her to reconstruct relationships with the others in the team.

This is a story with a happy ending: two years later, Gwendolyn became the leader of her team, with a seat at the executive table. Today, she coaches young leaders, focusing especially on those who feel like they aren't being seen, heard, or understood.

Gwendolyn's story is proof that being reflective is the most empowering resource available for professional development. Reflection forces an inside-out perspective. Gwendolyn went from ascribing her experiences to external parties and accepting her own part in creating those experiences. She could then enact change—by starting on the inside.

Are you inspired by Gwendolyn's story? Here are four practical reflection questions to engage with to strengthen your ability to pause and maintain your authentic presence:

- What stirs your certainty in a belief that fuels mistrust of another's relationship with you, seeing you as less than whole, resourceful, capable, and creative?

- What fuels your fear of silence and the discomfort of allowing another's independent thought to emerge?

- What self-trust becomes essential in surrendering to curiosity on behalf of another person without condition?

- What resourcefulness do you possess that reminds you of your privilege, and fulfills your responsibility, to witness another being express their full potency?

Inviting Change from Your Authentic Self

Change has a bad rap. People are much brainwashed into believing that change is hard. In fact, change can happen in an instant. It's the negotiating of life, recognizing that we want to change and then wondering how to change, that feels so burdensome and weighty. But change itself is always happening—in nature all around us, for instance, and even within us. We usually just don't notice it.

In the business world, change is also a constant—and there is a sense that change is occurring ever more rapidly, thanks to evolving technologies like generative artificial intelligence (AI), which progresses exponentially as it receives more data. That perception of rapidity can make us want to act and react quickly. It discourages us from taking pause—when, in fact, pause is what we need to navigate the changes around us and within us and the related tensions.

Tensions are always operating inside of you. To invite change and become comfortable with those tensions, you must also start on the inside. That means looking inward instead of outward, at the point of action. It requires an interior attention and ultimately making a declaration: "I'm accepting responsibility for the inner authority to choose how I'm relating to my life. And I can't do that if I don't know the essence of who I am—my authentic self."

EXERCISE: WHO *ARE* YOU, REALLY?

Reclaiming the authentic self often starts with revisiting your core values. It's a simple, practical way to retune your instrument and figure out who you are and what makes you sing. Take a moment to reflect on the values that you've always held near and dear. Do they still ring true today? Or have they shifted? Jot down your values.

Now, are you living those values? What actions allow you to breathe them into your everyday existence? These could be things you're doing now—or, if you aren't doing them now, things that you could be doing in the future.

Finally, how will you make space for those practices in your life going forward? Remember, the authentic self is rooted in practice. Practice is what will bring you back to your values, again and again, keeping your instrument tuned to the key you desire—to your authentic self. If your authentic self is a plant, practice is how you water it.

CHAPTER 8

INVITE CHANGE

An organization's ability to learn, and translate that learning into action rapidly, is the ultimate competitive advantage.
—JACK WELCH, AMERICAN EXECUTIVE

T o invite change is a sovereign choice, one that begins with reclaiming the authentic self. That requires recognizing that *you* are in charge of the experience you have of your life. That becomes the gift that keeps on giving—a gift you can bestow on both yourself and others. If you can shift your stance to worry less about whether people will accept you and instead invite them to meet you, that's a game changer.

I have worked with hundreds of C-suite leaders over my career, and, regardless of industry or background, they share one common worry, one that keeps many up at night: how to get sound and valuable decisions from leaders and their teams in a timely way. Why? A lack of good decision-making is expensive, interfering with innovation and productivity—and, in the process, hampering customer satisfaction, market share, and, finally, gross revenue.

The answer is to create a workplace environment that rewards people for accepting responsibility for following their inner authority for how they choose to show up, interact, and make decisions. This is how engagement is sustained and response-agility realized. This is how innovation finds the light. Most importantly, this is how *people* thrive, and people, with all their many diverse talents, are needed for any organization to stand the test of time.

Invite change from your authentic self, and you will begin to invite others on the journey with you. Change then becomes not intimidating but a valuable resource for fulfillment, whether in the workplace or for your personal quality of life. When we approach change from a place of sovereignty, we are no longer the victim of external circumstances controlling us. We control our own future. A line from the poem "Invictus," written by English poet William Ernest Henley, and often recited by Nelson Mandela, comes to mind: "I am the master of my fate, I am the captain of my soul."

Your Sovereignty Nurtures Everyone's Accountability

Sovereignty is the quality of accepting responsibility for our inner authority to choose how we relate with the circumstances of our own lives. When we take our life into our own hands, we also take it upon ourselves to act with integrity and gain response-agility with our life, our family, our community, our fellow human beings, and the planet as a whole. The idea of "accepting responsibility" speaks to accountability—in this case, your accountability to yourself. When you embrace this self-accountability through sovereignty, you open the door for others to do the same.

The idea of "holding others accountable" has gained ground in recent years, with leaders seeking employees who enthusiastically accept responsibility for what leaders request of them. When employees fail on this point, leaders become frustrated. The wasted emotional energy and drain on productivity—seen in repercussions like chasing after missed deadlines or resolving team member conflicts—make a lack of accountability a pricey problem to resolve.

The answer lies in sovereignty. I propose the concept "Team Sovereignty," a means of interacting that creates emotional health and a sense of belonging. Four simple questions can help create sovereignty within the team, favoring a collaborative rather than a transactional attitude:

- What brought you here?

- What is the team expected to deliver?

- What agreements are necessary for you to accept responsibility?

- How would you like to approach delivering the expectation while honoring the agreements made between us?

Start with a simple question that opens up the conversation to receive what each person chooses to make important to share with colleagues. Each team member must experience being seen and heard for their role and desired contribution. This creates a shared dialogue in the team setting, building credibility between members and creating discussions about shared purpose. How team members participate in terms of attitude and mood will become contagious and generate a field of experience that is highly influential.

This coalescing of people around shared purpose is more important than ever because the complexities we face in the workplace are greater than ever. As a leader, you probably tend to be future oriented, always thinking, *What's coming next?* I've got news for you: the future is now. We've got an explosion of new technologies shaking up entire industries. We've got a massively dissatisfied workforce. We've got Diversity, Equity, Inclusion, Justice, and Belonging (DEIJB) issues that have been somewhat brought to the light but remain largely unresolved.

The challenges of the modern workplace are too complex for any one person to solve alone. This is why leaders must create work environments rooted in continuous learning and collaboration—two things required to grapple with current and future challenges. What usually gets in the way of continuous learning? People holding onto their identity and not being led to experience rewarded vulnerability.

Without vulnerability, you can't create the level of connection that produces original thinking—a requirement of innovation, something organizations need if they are to overcome the challenges of the future/now. Similarly, genuine collaboration only becomes possible when everyone feels safe as their authentic self. This is what allows them to show up in sovereignty, to engage meaningfully, communicate clearly, and act productively.

> **The challenges of the modern workplace are too complex for any one person to solve alone.**

Generative AI is the perfect example of this. It's proof that no one person can know the whole story by themselves. It's such a complex and unwieldy subject; it simply can't be wrangled by any one individual, no matter how intelligent they are. For a tool like ChatGPT to function effectively, linguists must work with writers, who work with software engineers, who work with indexers, who work with beta testers. The list goes on. Meanwhile, these tools are learning themselves, gaining new abilities without human intervention—becoming generative in ways humans did not anticipate. This is yet another testament to the fact that no one person is able to fully comprehend this topic, much less manage it, alone.

In this modern world, the idea of collaboration is no longer an aspiration, but it's a requirement. Leaders must learn to engage with others with a learner's mindset, accepting that they can't be an expert in everything. Intellectually, most leaders understand that. However, they often fail to embody that belief in practice. They may steamroll their teammates (think of Ricardo's story) or mother them (remember Maria's story). But they do not invite them to show up authentically, as their true selves, and collaborate in a meaningful way—with sovereignty. This pattern must be broken, and that starts with leadership.

The Responsibility Lies with You

At the beginning of this book, I noted that tension in the workplace is inevitable—and suggested that the intensity of that tension, and the frequency with which thorny problems arise, is growing. This book is all about where leaders get stuck when navigating those tensions and problems. With the term "leaders," I'm not speaking exclusively to those in formal leadership roles. In my mind, everyone is a leader— because leading well starts with leading *yourself* well. In the end, it boils down to one thing: it starts with you. You must accept responsibility to self-lead. If you *are* in a formal leadership role, you can then lead others more effectively.

This requires pausing to reflect. It requires noticing. It requires putting emotionality aside. And therein lies the problem: too often, our emotions overtake us, and we tend to get reactive, to make snap judgments and rapid-response decisions (remember Gwendolyn's story).

But what if you broke the pattern and reacted differently? What if you paused and held the tension and then utilized it to explore an alternative avenue, one you might not have even considered had you acted immediately?

Experiment with something different. Try something new. That is essentially all I am asking you to do. You don't have to stick with the alternative route or response you explore. Just try it and be open to allowing something else to show itself. You can decide later whether it's worthy or not, depending on how it compares to other options you've explored in the past or might consider in the future. Give your mind something to work with that goes beyond its usual habit and preference. Try to break the status quo.

In the process, you will invite change—a change not only in how you approach a thorny problem but, just as importantly, a change in yourself. Hopefully, this shift will allow you to become nearer to your authentic self, what we might call your best self: the most finely aligned version of yourself. You will then invite others to do the same, becoming the kind of leader who doesn't create apathy but inspires— the kind of leader who is capable of being their best selves while encouraging others to do the same.

EXERCISE: REFLECT, IDENTIFY JUDGMENT, AND RECONSTRUCT

Throughout this book, you've done a series of exercises designed to help you reclaim your authentic self, regain sovereignty, examine judgment, and better tolerate the presence of tension. The end goal has been Generative Wholeness™, a vehicle to leading well—with the vehicle for this wholeness being a car, or ACAAR. I'd now like you to put together the pieces for yourself and go through the full ACAAR exercise in one sitting, from start to finish. I suggest you set aside twenty minutes for this exercise.

You've noticed a situation, an initiative, or a key stakeholder relationship that continually stimulates your impatience. Use this noticing as your opportunity to hit pause, and practice shifting your mindset toward greater patience.

Awareness

Remember the beginning of the process. Now, notice what data, information, experience, or perspectives were dismissed or discounted—and now seem relevant for a new, more empowering choice.

Clarity

Notice the internal motivation or stimulus for wanting to make those choices. This is often a belief.

Alignment

Think to the beginning of the process. Consider what the basis was for choosing those actions that didn't produce the result you expected. The basis is often a value or principle. The four questions in the following diagram offer a way to surface what motivated those chosen actions to begin understanding how mindset can operate quite invisibly. Answer all four, in any order you'd like.

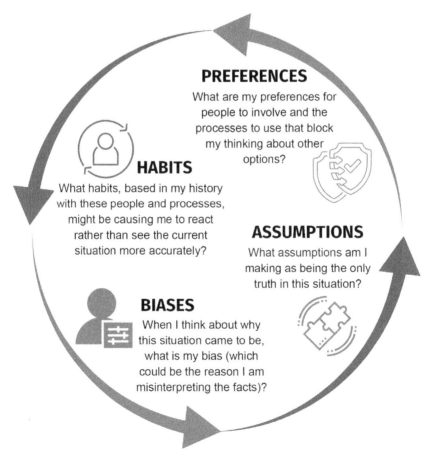

1. What are my preferences for people to involve and the processes to use that block my thinking about other options?

2. What habits, based on my history with these people and processes, might be causing me to react rather than see the current situation more accurately?

3. What assumptions am I making as being the only truth in this situation?

4. When I think about why this situation came to be, what is my bias (which could be the reason I am misinterpreting the facts)?

Through the lens of your new awareness, use this step-by-step method to choose the beliefs or principles that you now understand as the most important drivers—those drivers that fully align with decision-making criteria for your teams as they pursue new choices and produce new, better results.

Action

Identify the actions that produced the new desirable result.

Result

Describe what the new satisfactory result is.

CONCLUSION

When I was on the Thought Leadership Institute Board for the International Coaching Federation in 2020 and 2021, we met with about thirty researchers from around the globe, bringing them together in conversation. The outcomes of those discussions were summarized in a peer-reviewed paper, "The Grand Challenge for Research on the Future of Coaching," published in the *Journal of Applied Behavioral Science.*[25]

Following that publication, I was asked to join a cohort at Royal Roads University in Canada, speaking to candidates who were earning their master's degrees in research in the field of executive and organizational coaching. They were there for their residential week, and I was participating on the last day of that week. I was anticipating some malaise and exhaustion as I went into it. After all, they'd been hard at work all week. My assumptions were quickly proven wrong.

The evening before I came on, the group had done an activity trying to formulate their purpose statement for being a researcher. I decided to build on that. So, I took them through an experiential activity. I invited each person to answer a simple question quietly,

---

25   Richard E. Boyatzis, Alicia Hullinger, Sharon F. Ehasz, Janet M. Harvey, Silvia Tassa-rotti, Anna Gallotti, and Frances Penafort, "The Grand Challenge for Research on the Future of Coaching," *The Journal of Applied Behavioral Science* 58 (2022): 202–222, https://doi.org/10.1177/0021886322107993.

capturing a few notes that told their story as a researcher—what they heard in their head, their heart, and their gut in answering this question: "What stops you from living and identifying fully as a researcher?"

After a couple minutes, each person turned to a partner and shared what their reflection time surfaced. Even through the video screen, the buzz in the room could be felt. After a few minutes, I invited them to return their attention internally, allowing the conversation they'd just had to vibrate within themselves for a minute. Then, I asked them to write their purpose statement for being a researcher below their notes about what stops them from this path/identity, read all of it quietly, and notice any changes in their internal vibration. To my delight, this series of reflection steps totally rocked the room.

I then took it a step further and had one person come up on stage with me. I had them sit in a chair in front of everybody, while I worked with them in a coaching capacity. People don't usually love exposing their vulnerabilities in an auditorium full of people, so I didn't anticipate many volunteers—but after that first person went, the next one raised their hand. And the next. And the next.

By the end of the session, nine people had come up and willingly sat in that chair to discuss their personal reflection and their purpose in becoming a researcher. All kinds of tender points were revealed, from individuals worrying that they lacked the confidence needed for the career path they'd chosen to others stressing about practical components, such as publication records and connections. These individuals had chosen to go down the path of research for many distinct reasons; their worries as to why they might not be able to live up to their chosen title, *researcher*, were just as diverse.

Throughout, I asked questions that would help each of them start to dismantle the hurdles they perceived to being a researcher.

Together, we unveiled the mental barriers and emotional blinders that kept them from believing they could be a researcher who would be useful to the world. They all had these big visions about being a researcher and why they wanted to do it and what it entailed. But that vision was often not grounded in reality. And then they'd stop themselves, because they'd think maybe it was just a fantasy. So, it was largely a question of shifting that idea of what it meant to be a researcher. With a few people, we helped them to shift their point of view about the research question they were working on, taking steps to make it more relatable or more grounded in reality.

It was a live, spontaneous experience of people sitting in their discomfort in a very vulnerable way and then not only exploring that discomfort in an open conversation but also holding it, just a little bit longer. For many of them, that extra moment of pause made the difference. That was what allowed a bit of wonder to bubble up so that they could open their minds to different routes to take. It all began with a moment of pause.

If you take away nothing else from this book, I hope you take away that—the value of pause. Remember, pause creates more time than it takes. And the wondrous possibilities that pause can open for you are well worth exploring.

If this book has sparked something in you—curiosity, wonder, judgment, irritation, joy, whatever the case may be—I invite you to visit inviteCHANGE.com to learn more. You'll find additional exercises, articles, and case studies that can help you in your own journey toward reclaiming your authentic self and inviting change.

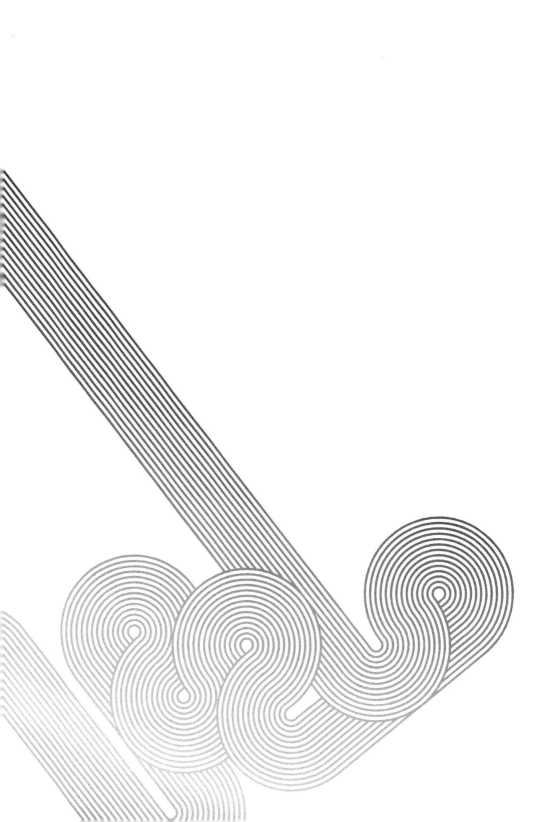

ABOUT THE AUTHOR

JANET M. HARVEY is a vanguard thinker, speaker, author, and the CEO of inviteCHANGE, a coaching and human development organization that shapes a world where people love their life's work. With nearly thirty years of executive experience, Janet passionately believes in liberating each leader's potential to optimize organizational performance.

Janet holds a Bachelor of Science degree in Economics with a minor in Finance from San Francisco State University, as well as a Master of Arts degree in Organizational Development and Human Resource Management from the University of San Francisco. She is also an International Coaching Federation, ICF, credentialed Master Certified Coach, with twelve-thousand-plus hours of experience, primarily in organizational and executive leadership engagements.

Janet served as a board director for the ICF Thought Leadership Institute (2020 and 2021), on the ICF Global Enterprise Board (2009–2013), as the ICF Global President in 2012, and as the Chair for the ICF Foundation Board (2010–2015).

This is Janet's second book. Her previous book, *Invite Change: Lessons from 2020, The Year of No Return*, is available for purchase on Amazon.

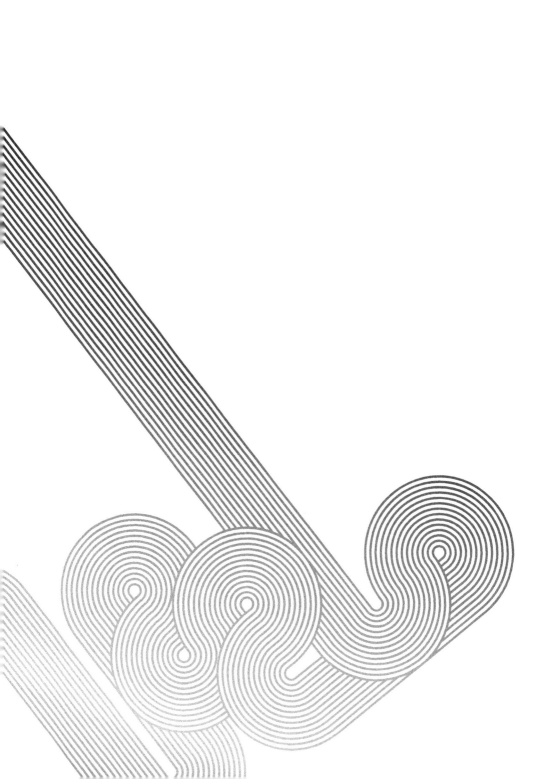

CONTACT

You are invited! Join our virtual community and access a variety of free resources to continue and deepen your learning. And, to purchase more books for your team, your organization, and your friends and family, you can find this book at these places:

janetmharvey.com | invitechange.com

Contact Information

Connect with me and share your experience of reading, and more important applying what you learn.

And a BONUS: If you buy a book for another, let me know that and share your address and I'll send you another one signed, so you can also give away your first copy!

Email: janet@janetmharvey.com

LinkedIn: https://www.linkedin.com/in/janetharvey/

Website: https://www.janetmharvey.com and https://www.inviteCHANGE.com

Key Services Available

I am obsessed with helping leaders who lead for humanity to thrive.

- Generative Coaching for Individuals

- Generative Coaching for Teams

- Keynote Speaking and Workshops for Leaders and Teams

    - Sustain Excellence through Generative Wholeness™

    - 90 Days to 10X Productivity ~ The Generative Vehicle for Change

    - Sovereign Living Generates Sovereign Leading for a Thriving Humanity